Trees

OF BRITAIN AND EUROPE

GREEN GUIDE

Trees

OF BRITAIN AND EUROPE

bob press

ILLUSTRATED BY colin emberson

NEW HOLLAND

This edition first published in the UK in 2001 by
New Holland Publishers (UK) Ltd
Garfield House, 86-88 Edgware Road, London W2 2EA

www.newhollandpublishers.com

9 10

ISBN   1 85974 927 5

Phototypeset by AKM Associates (UK) Ltd
Reproduction by Scantrans Pte Ltd
Printed and bound in Singapore by
Kyodo Printing Co (Singapore) Pte Ltd

Contents

Introduction

Trees are a major feature of any landscape, whether massed together in forests and woods or as isolated individuals. As well as being things of beauty, they bring a sense of scale and permanence to their surroundings and mark the cycle of the seasons. Trees play a vital role in maintaining and protecting our environment. They prevent erosion, are part of the living system that recycles water, oxygen and carbon dioxide into the atmosphere, and provide habitats and food for many other organisms. Some have great economic value, mainly as timber or fruit trees but also as decorative ornamentals.

The extensive forests that once covered most of Europe are now either gone or greatly reduced, many felled and cleared in ancient times to make way for agriculture. This is especially true of the broad-leaved evergreen forests of southern Europe. In the less densely populated regions of the far north more forests have survived. In modern times, re-afforestation programmes have led to large areas of land being returned to forest, although the trees planted are often not native but foreign species which yield useful timber.

Approximately 250 species of tree are native to Europe, many of them rare or of restricted distribution. Through the centuries many more species have been introduced from elsewhere. Some of these are restricted to parks and gardens, others are planted on a commercial scale or have escaped into the wild to spread and become completely naturalised. This concise guide describes the 150 most commonly encountered species, whether native or introduced, wild or planted in streets, parks or forestry developments.

How to Identify Trees

Plants differ from one another in many ways and trees are no exception. With experience, identifying trees is relatively straightforward but for the beginner it can be confusing. One of the greatest problems is that, unlike wild flowers, most parts of trees are frequently out of reach. The following notes give some idea of which features to look for, and explain some of the terms used in the descriptions and keys. When you encounter a tree you wish to identify, examine it carefully, noting the various features. The key to species on page 15 will help you decide to which species or group of species it belongs. Always take the book to the tree; never break off parts or otherwise damage it. Wounds may become infected and eventually kill the tree.

Trees are woody plants with a single, clearly defined stem or trunk branching well above ground level. Shrubs differ in being smaller, with a more diffuse shape and several stems or a trunk which branches close to ground level. However, many trees can be short and shrubby and a large number of so-called shrubs may reach considerable size, so the distinction is rather artificial. Some trees produce young stems or suckers at or near the base of the trunk.

Bark forms the protective outer layer of the trunk and branches and can be thin and smooth or thick, rough and corky. It splits as the tree grows, cracking or peeling away to be constantly replaced by new bark. The pattern of cracks and the colour of the bark or of the areas revealed as it falls can be useful recognition features.

The twigs and branches make up the crown of the tree. The overall shape of the crown can vary between trees of different species, and between those of the same species but of different ages. Young cedars, for example, are conical but old ones are flat-topped and spreading. In general, young conifers have a very regular pattern of branching while young broad-leaved trees branch more randomly. Palms are unusual in having no branches. The crown is composed solely of leaves crowded at the top of the trunk.

An obvious distinction is between deciduous and evergreen trees. Deciduous trees shed all their leaves annually. In Europe this occurs in autumn, when the dying leaves may exhibit a striking range of colours, mainly shades of yellow, orange and red. New leaves are produced each spring. Evergreens also shed their leaves but more gradually, constantly replacing them so that there is always a full crown of foliage.

Stipules are leaf-like growths at the base of the leaf stalk. They are present in a number of species but often fall early.

Leaf Types

Needle-like (Pines)

Scale-like (Cypresses)

Lance-shaped (Willows)

Pinnately lobed (Oaks)

Pinnately divided (Rowans)

Palmately divided (Chestnuts)

Introduction

The shape and arrangement of the leaves are often characteristic of particular trees. Most have leaves alternating on the shoot but some have opposite pairs or whorls of leaves. The leaves may be divided into leaflets. Pinnate leaves have the leaflets in two parallel rows and sometimes a leaflet at the tip. Palmate leaves have the leaflets radiating from the leaf stalk like the fingers of a hand. Similarly, the leaves may be pinnately or palmately lobed without being completely divided into leaflets. The leaf margin may be entire, i.e. unbroken, or variously toothed. Leaves also vary in colour, texture and hairiness. They are generally paler and more hairy on the underside. Conifers have leathery leaves which are either narrow and needle-like or scale-like, overlapping and pressed against the shoot. Most, but not all, are evergreen.

Flowers are made up of sepals, petals, stamens and ovaries. Petals and sepals provide most clues to identity, especially their number, size and colour. Where the sepals and petals are indistinguishable from one another, they are referred to as *perianth segments*. Stamens are the male parts of the flower, ovaries are the female parts, and flowers may be male, female or both, when they are known as *hermaphrodite*. Male and female flowers are sometimes borne in separate clusters or even on separate trees. The flowers may be solitary or grouped in a variety of clusters, spikes or heads. Wind-pollinated trees have tiny flowers massed in distinctive, slender catkins. Conifers have male and female cones instead of flowers and fruits. Male cones are yellow when shedding pollen but it is the large female cones which are most noticeable. When ripe they are generally woody but can be fleshy and berry-like as in Junipers.

Fruits of non-coniferous trees fall into two broad categories, fleshy and juicy or dry. Fleshy and juicy fruits include all berries and berry-like fruits as well as firm fruits such as apples. Dry fruits include pods, capsules and nuts.

Families of Trees

The species in this book are grouped into 40 families whose essential characteristics are described here.

Ginkgo and Yew Ginkgo has deciduous, fan-shaped leaves. Yew has evergreen needles. Both have fleshy, berry-like fruits.

Cypresses All are evergreen trees or shrubs. Most have overlapping, scale-like leaves but some Junipers have needles as well as or instead of scale-leaves. Cones are globular, with scales touching edge to edge; in Junipers they are fleshy.

Swamp-cypresses Deciduous trees with needles. Cone globular.

Pines Evergreen or deciduous trees with needles in bundles with a sheathing base. Cones are egg-shaped.

Willows Deciduous trees or shrubs. The alternate leaves often have large stipules at the base of the leaf stalk. Flowers lack a perianth and are borne in male and female catkins on separate trees. Seeds are tufted with white hairs.

Walnuts Deciduous trees which exude latex from broken twigs. Leaves are pinnately divided. Flowers are in separate male and female catkins on the same tree; males lack a perianth.

Birches and Hazels Deciduous trees or shrubs with broad, alternate leaves. The flowers, in separate male and female catkins, lack a perianth. In Birches the small winged nutlets are borne in cone-like catkins. Hazels have large, woody nuts, each attached to a leafy, ragged or lobed involucre.

Beeches and Oaks Deciduous or evergreen trees with alternate, often lobed or spiny leaves. Flowers are small, the males in catkins, the females in clusters of 1–3. Nuts or nut-like fruits are partly or wholly enclosed in a scaly or spiny cup.

Elms Deciduous trees. The alternate leaves are often markedly asymmetrical at the base. Small flowers are either all hermaphrodite or with some males. Seeds are surrounded by a papery wing.

Magnolias Evergreen trees or shrubs with alternate, entire leaves. Large, solitary flowers have 5 or more perianth segments.

Laurels and Mulberries Laurels have evergreen, entire leaves. Mulberries are deciduous with toothed or deeply lobed leaves. Sometimes male and female flowers are borne on separate trees. There are 4 perianth segments. In Fig the flowers are tiny and enclosed in a fleshy receptacle. Fruit is berry-like.

Planes and Maples Deciduous trees with often peeling bark and mostly deeply palmately lobed leaves. Leaves are alternate in Planes, paired in Maples. Planes have 4–6-petalled flowers in separate male and female, globular heads and seeds with a tuft of hairs at the base. Maples usually have 5-petalled hermaphrodite flowers; winged fruits form pairs.

Roses Deciduous or evergreen trees or shrubs. The alternate leaves are entire, lobed or pinnately divided. Usually showy flowers are 5-petalled. Fruit is fleshy and firm or juicy, with one to several, often stony, seeds.

Peas Deciduous or evergreen trees, often with pinnately divided leaves. Petals 5, often unequal. Fruit is a dry, slender pod with few to many seeds.

Citruses and Hollies Evergreen trees. Citruses have spiny twigs, Hollies have spiny leaves. The flowers are white and fragrant, 5-petalled in Citruses, 4-petalled and with males and females on

Introduction

separate trees in Hollies. Fruit is a berry, that of Citruses with a leathery rind.

Quassias and Sumachs Deciduous or evergreen trees or shrubs, with pinnately divided leaves. Five-petalled flowers are borne in large, often branched clusters. The fruit is small, berry-like, that of Quassias dry and with a long wing.

Horse-chestnuts Large deciduous trees. Leaves are palmately divided into leaflets. Large flowers have 4–5 petals and long, curved stamens. Fruit is one to several nuts in a spiny case.

Spindles and Boxes Spindles are deciduous, Boxes evergreen. The leaves and twigs are paired. Inconspicuous flowers are 4-petalled or lack a perianth; Boxes have separate male and female flowers. Fruit is a capsule.

Buckthorns and Oleasters Small, deciduous trees or shrubs, frequently spiny or thorny. Leaves are paired or alternate. Flowers are hermaphrodite or males and females on separate trees; those of Oleasters have 2 or 4 sepals only, those of Buckthorns have 4 or 5 petals. Fruit is berry-like or a hard nut.

Limes Deciduous trees with alternate, heart-shaped leaves. Fragrant, 5-petalled flowers hang in clusters beneath a wing-like bract. Fruit is a small nut.

Tamarisks Small, slender trees or shrubs with wand-like twigs and tiny, scale-like, clasping leaves.

Myrtles Evergreen trees with peeling, shredding or fibrous bark and highly aromatic leaves. Leaves are of two kinds: juveniles are paired and often blue; adult leaves are alternate and dull green. The perianth segments are fused to form a lid which falls when the flower opens. Fruit is a woody capsule.

Pomegranates and Dogwoods Small deciduous trees or shrubs. Leaves are paired and entire. Pomegranate flowers are large, and have 5–7 petals. Dogwoods have small, clustered flowers with 4 petals. Fruit is a berry, that of Pomegranate with a leathery rind.

Heaths Evergreen trees with alternate, toothed leaves. Flowers are urn-shaped. Fruit is a warty berry.

Olives Evergreen or deciduous trees or shrubs. Leaves are paired and either entire or pinnately divided into toothed leaflets. Petals, if present, are 4, joined in a tube. Fruit is either a berry or dry and winged.

Bignonias and Figworts Deciduous trees with large, paired leaves. Flowers are tubular and 5-petalled. Pod-like fruit is short in Figworts, long in Bignonias.

Honeysuckles and Viburnums Small trees or shrubs, evergreen or deciduous. Paired leaves are pinnately divided, deeply lobed or undivided. Five-petalled flowers borne in large clusters. Fruit is a berry.

Agaves and Palms Evergreen trees with a single straight or forked trunk but no branches. Leaves are large, sword-shaped in Agaves, fan- or feather-shaped in Palms, and all crowded at the top of the trunk.

The Tree Keys

The key to species is biased towards leaf characteristics as they are most easily observed. Fruits are also included, as those of trees tend to be obvious and often long-lasting; they can frequently be found on the ground around the tree. When examining fruits or other parts not actually attached to the tree, be sure they do come from the tree in question and not from neighbouring, and possibly different, trees.

Every step in the key consists of two contrasting statements. Look at your tree and see which is true. The next numbered stage is indicated at the end of the line. Follow the series of correct statements until you arrive at a name and page number or numbers where you can check your identification. The first key will lead you to secondary keys, and these to species. Sometimes a tree will fit both statements. These few species are keyed out twice, so it does not matter which statement you choose. After using the key to decide which species your tree is, turn to the appropriate page and use the description and illustrations to confirm your selection. Even if you find the key a little daunting at first, persevere. It is an essential identification tool.

Key to Species

1 Crown of leaves only, in a single tuft at tip of trunk   Key 1
  Crown of leafy branches   **2**
2 Leaves either needle- or scale-like   Key 2
  Leaves broader, not scale-like   **3**
3 Leaves in opposite pairs on shoots   Key 3
  Leaves alternate on shoots   **4**
4 Leaves divided into separate leaflets   Key 4
  Leaves simple or lobed but not divided into leaflets   **5**
5 Leaves evergreen   Key 5
  Leaves deciduous   **6**
6 Fruit fleshy or juicy   Key 6
  Fruit dry   Key 7

Key 1

1 Leaves undivided, sword-shaped; trunk often forked
                              Cabbage-tree   95
  Leaves divided; trunk unbranched   **2**
2 Leaves feathery, pinnate   Canary Island Date Palm   96
  Leaves fan-shaped, palmate   **3**
3 Tree up to 14m high   Chinese Windmill Palm   96
  Tree rarely more than 2m high   European Fan Palm   95

Key 2

Key 3

Key 4

1	Leaves palmate, leaflets radiating from leaf stalk		**2**
	Leaves pinnate, leaflets in 2 rows		**3**
2	Leaflets 3	Laburnum	72
	Leaflets 5–7	Horse-chestnut	79
3	Leaves twice-pinnate	Silver Wattle	71
	Leaves once-pinnate		**4**
4	Young twigs densely velvet-hairy	Stag's-horn Sumach	75
	Young twigs not velvet-hairy		**5**
5	Evergreen		**6**
	Deciduous		**7**
6	Leaves aromatic; fruit nut- or bead-like	Pepper-tree	75
		Mastic-tree	76
	Leaves not aromatic; fruit a long pod	Carob	70
7	Twigs thorny; flowers pea-like	False Acacia	73
	Twigs not thorny; flowers not pea-like		**8**
8	Flowers in catkins or unbranched clusters; cut twigs leaking latex	Walnuts	42
	Flowers in large branched clusters; cut twigs not leaking latex		**9**
9	Flowers white; fruit berry-like	True Service-tree	59
		Rowan	59
	Flowers greenish or brown; fruit dry		**10**
10	Twigs sticky; fruit nut-like	Turpentine-tree	76
	Twigs not sticky; fruit winged	Tree-of-Heaven	74

Key 5

1	Leaves spiny		**2**
	Leaves sometimes toothed but not spiny		**3**
2	Fruit an acorn; flowers green, males in catkins	Oaks	48–9
	Fruit a berry; flowers white, in clusters	Holly	80
3	Leaves with rusty hairs beneath		**4**
	Leaves smooth beneath		**7**
4	Leaves toothed, flowers *c* 10mm	Loquat	61
	Leaves entire, flowers up to 250mm	Evergreen Magnolia	55
5	Leaf stalk winged; twigs spiny	Sweet Orange	73
		Lemon	74
	Leaf stalk not winged; twigs not spiny		**6**
6	Leaf margin wavy or rolled under; fruit a berry		**7**
	Leaf margin neither wavy nor rolled under; fruit dry		**8**
7	Leaves smelling of bay, margin wavy	Sweet Bay	56
	Leaves smelling of almonds, margin rolled under		
		Cherry Laurel	69
8	Leaves smelling of eucalyptus; fruit a woody capsule	Gums	86–7
	Leaves not aromatic; fruit a long pod	Golden Wreath	71
		Blackwood	72

Key 6

Key 7

1	Twigs zig-zag, spiny	Christ's Thorn 81
	Twigs not zig-zag or spiny	**2**
2	Leaves lobed	**3**
	Leaves not lobed	**6**
3	Leaves cut square or notched at tip; flowers large, up to 50mm	Tulip-tree 55
	Leaves rounded or pointed at tip, flowers small, in clusters or catkins	**4**
4	Leaves pinnately lobed; fruit an acorn	Oaks 47, 49–51
	Leaves palmately or irregularly lobed; seeds silky plumed	**5**
5	Leaves white-felted below	White Poplar 40
	Leaves smooth or sparsely hairy below	London Plane 56
6	Flowers in cylindrical catkins	**7**
	Flowers single or in clusters	**13**
7	Male and female flowers in same catkin, fruit spiny	Sweet Chestnut 47
	Male and female flowers in separate catkins, fruit not spiny	**8**
8	Fruit a capsule releasing silky-plumed seeds	**9**
	Fruit a nut or winged nutlet	**10**
9	Leaves broadly oval to heart-shaped, bluntly toothed	Poplars 40–1
	Leaves usually tapering to a long point, entire or sharply toothed	Willows 36–9
10	Nut enveloped in a leafy involucre	**11**
	Nutlets winged, in cone-like catkins	**12**
11	Nut single or in small clusters	Hazel 46
	Nuts in long catkins	Hornbeam 45
		Hop-hornbeam 45
12	Fruiting catkins cylindrical, pendulous	Birches 43
	Fruiting catkins oval, not pendulous	Alders 44
13	Leaves entire	**14**
	Leaves toothed	**15**
14	Leaves oval to elliptical; nutlets in a spiny case; flowers yellowish	Beech 46
	Leaves almost circular; seeds in a long pod; flowers pink	Judas-tree 70
15	Leaves asymmetric at base; each seed surrounded by a papery wing	Elms 51–3
	Leaves symmetrical at base; fruit cluster attached to a single, wing-like bract	Limes 83–4

Ginkgos

Maidenhair-tree *Ginkgo biloba*
Up to 30m. The fan-shaped
leaves both look and feel
extremely leathery and pliant.
Irregularly conical tree with
one or more trunks. Shoots
either long with widely spaced
leaves or short spur-like, with
clusters of leaves. Leaves 120 x
100mm, notched, fan-shaped
with radiating veins. Flowers
March–April, males and
females on separate trees;
males in thick, erect catkins,
females singly or in pairs, on
long stalks. Fruit 25–30mm,
fleshy, oval, yellowish when
ripe; smells unpleasant;
contains a single stony seed.
Native to China but probably
extinct in the wild; widely
planted in parks and gardens
in Europe.

Yew *Taxus baccata* Up to 25m.
Sprays of dark, dull needles
contrast with reddish bark
and matt scarlet berry-like
fruit. Evergreen tree or shrub
with thick trunk and rounded
crown. Bark flaking and
peeling. Needles 10-30mm,
flattened, sharp-pointed;
spirally arranged on the twig
but spread out to form two
lateral rows; dark green
above, yellowish beneath.
Flowers February–April, males
and females on separate trees;
males yellow, females
greenish. Fruit consists of a
seed 6-7mm long surrounded
by fleshy, cup-like aril up to
10mm long. Shade tolerant,
common in woods and scrub,
especially on limestone,
throughout Europe.

Lawson-cypress *Chamaecyparis lawsoniana* Up to 45m. Flattened sprays of foliage and a nodding leading shoot give this dense evergreen tree a drooping appearance. Shoots parsley-scented, light green, forming flattened, pendulous sprays. Leaves tiny, scale-like, 2mm long, closely pressed against the shoot in alternating pairs; those on upper side dark green, those on lower with whitish marks. Cones 8mm diameter, bluish-green and resembling footballs; made up of 8 scales, each with a ridge in a central depression and ripening pale brown. Native to western North America, widely planted in Europe and sometimes naturalised.

Monterey Cypress *Cupressus macrocarpa* Up to 35m. The markedly upswept branches of this evergreen tree bear ropey or cord-like foliage. Crown narrow and pointed when young but broadly domed in old trees. Bark yellowish-brown, ridged. Leaves 1–2mm, blunt and scaly, pressed against the shoot in alternating pairs. Cones 20–30mm diameter, resemble footballs composed of 8–14 scales, each scale with a pointed central boss; initially green, ripening shiny brown in second year. Native to southern California; salt-resistant and favoured for coastal shelter and ornamental plantings in western and southern Europe.

Cypresses

Italian Cypress *Cupressus sempervirens* Up to 30m. Low and spreading in its wild form, this evergreen has a more commonly seen cultivated form making a dense, spire-like tree with sharply upswept branches giving a narrowly columnar crown. Bark greyish, often with spiral ridges. Leaves 0.5–1mm long, scaly and blunt; pressed against the shoot in alternating pairs. Cones 25–40mm diameter, ellipsoid-oblong with 8–14 scales, each scale with a short, blunt central point and often wavy at the edges; ripen from green to yellowish-grey in second year. Native to the Aegean; widely planted in southern Europe and naturalised in many places.

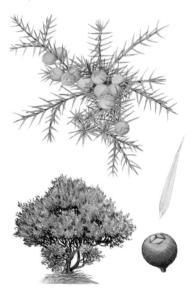

Juniper *Juniperus communis* Up to 6m. Prickly evergreen foliage becomes studded with dark, dull, berry-like fruits. Small tree or often only a low shrub. Bark reddish, shredding. Needles stiff, prickly, arranged in whorls of 3; bluish with a broad white band above. Cones 6–9mm, fleshy, oval to globular; initially green, they ripen blue-black with a dull bloom in the second or third year. Found scattered throughout Europe, especially on lime-rich soils, but mainly on mountains in the south.

Phoenician Juniper *Juniperus phoenicea* Up to 8m. An evergreen with foliage of two distinct kinds; cord-like shoots with scaly leaves, and young growth bearing needles. Small tree or sometimes a spreading shrub. Leaves of young growth up to 14mm long, needle-like, wide-spreading, in whorls of 3; scaly adult leaves are only 1mm long, blunt with pale margins and closely pressed to the shoot in pairs or threes. Cones 6–14mm, berry-like; blackish at first, becoming green then yellowish, finally ripening dark red in the second year. Widespread throughout coastal Mediterranean regions.

Western Red-cedar *Thuja plicata* Up to 65m. Otherwise closely resembling Lawson-cypress, this pyramidal or conical evergreen is very erect, leader and foliage never drooping. Tall tree, with stout trunk. Bark reddish, shredding. Foliage resin-scented, forms flattened sprays. Scale leaves 2–3mm, glossy green above, faintly marked with white below; pressed against the shoot in alternating pairs, lateral pairs larger than vertical pairs. Cones 12mm long, ovoid; 10–12 leafy, overlapping scales each with hook on inner side of tip; ripen green to brown. Native to western North America, planted in cool, damp parts of western and central Europe, sometimes naturalised.

25

Swamp-cypress *Taxodium distichum* Up to 50m. Clusters of stump-like, aerial roots usually grow up around the trunk of this deciduous tree. Conical to triangular or domed, with a fluted trunk and reddish, fibrous, peeling bark. Needles 8-20mm, pale green; flattened, pointed; spirally arranged on persistent long shoots but form two rows on the short deciduous side-shoots. Cones 12-30mm, globose with short, thick stalks; ripen purple. Cone-scales bluntly diamond-shaped, each with small, curved central spine. Native to swampy parts of south-eastern North America, often planted in similar soils in southern Europe for ornament and timber.

Common Silver-fir *Abies alba* Up to 50m. The spiky, ragged crown of this tall evergreen often overtops surrounding trees. Pyramidal to narrowly conical tree. Young twigs densely hairy. Needles 15-30mm x 1.5-2mm, flattened and slightly notched; blue-green, with two silvery bands below; lateral needles spread horizontally but shorter upper ones grow up and out, forming a distinct central parting down the shoot. Cones 100-200mm, erect, cylindrical, with a deflexed bract below each scale; green ripening to brown. Forms extensive natural forests in central Europe; from northern Spain to the Balkans; also planted for timber in northern and western Europe.

Caucasian Fir *Abies nordmanniana* Up to 70m. A dark and densely foliaged evergreen tree, retaining its branches almost to ground level, even in old age. Stout trunk and conical outline. Young twigs sparsely hairy. Needles 15-35mm x 1.5-2mm, flattened, with notched tips; dark green, two broad white bands on underside; they all curve up and forwards, not leaving a central parting down the shoot. Erect cones 100-200mm, cylindrical, with a long, deflexed bract beneath each scale; ripen dark brown. Native to mountain areas of north-east Turkey and the Caucasus but widely planted in central Europe and elsewhere for timber.

Grand Fir *Abies grandis* Up to 100m. A stout, fast-growing evergreen tree with a narrow, symmetrical, conical crown. Young twigs are olive green, with sparse, minute hairs. Needles are of various lengths, 20-60mm x 1.5-2mm, dark glossy green with two silvery bands below; flattened and notched, they spread out to either side of the shoot. Cones 50-100mm, dark brown; erect, cylindrical but taper at the tips. Bracts are concealed by cone-scales. A western North American species planted for timber in wet areas of northern and central Europe.

Pines

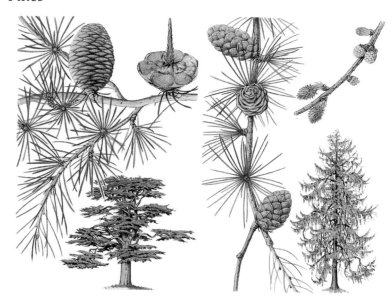

Cedar-of-Lebanon *Cedrus libani*
Up to 40m. Easily recognised
by the characteristic, flat,
shelf-like masses of foliage
developed by mature trees;
the crowns of young
specimens are conical.
Evergreen tree with massive
trunk supporting heavy,
horizontal branches. Needles
20–30mm, dark green, three-
sided; grow mostly in whorls
of 10–15 on spur-like short
shoots, singly on long shoots.
Cones 70–120mm, ripen from
purple to brown in autumn
the following year; erect,
barrel-shaped, breaking up to
leave the central spike
attached to the tree. Native to
south-west Asia; widely
planted as a pollution-
resistant ornamental and park
tree.

European Larch *Larix decidua*
Up to 35m. Larch woods take
on a yellowish hue in autumn
as the tufted needles turn
golden before falling. Conical,
deciduous tree. Bark grey to
pale brown. Pendulous shoots
are rough with old leaf bases.
Needles 12–30mm, pale green,
flattened, soft; borne mostly
in whorls of 30–40 on spur-like
short shoots, singly on long
shoots. Male cones yellow.
Female cones red when
young; oval, 20–30mm when
ripe; rounded, close-pressed
scales; stay on tree for several
years after seeds are shed.
Fast-growing, short-lived
mountain species from the
Alps and Carpathians, planted
for timber throughout
northern and central Europe.

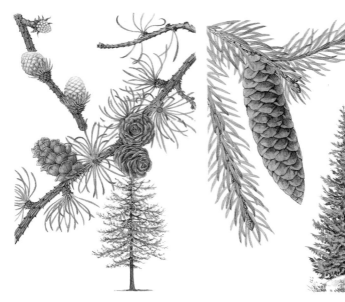

Japanese Larch *Larix kaempferi* Up to 40m. Blue-green in summer foliage, stands of Japanese Larch appear orange-brown in winter. Deciduous tree, broadly conical with widespreading branches and scaly, reddish-brown bark. Shoots orange-brown with a waxy bloom. Needles 15–30mm, flattened and borne mostly in whorls of about 40 on spur-like shoots; bluish- to greyish-green above with two white bands beneath. Male cones yellow, young females creamy-yellow with green bracts; ripe cones 15–35mm, oval, with rounded scales outwardly curved at tips; persist on the tree. Native to Japan but widespread as a timber tree in north-west Europe.

Norway Spruce *Picea abies* Up to 65m. Familiar as the Christmas tree, this evergreen has sweeping, curved branches, the upper ascending, the lower drooping. Conical tree with reddish-brown bark. Needles 10-25mm, four-sided, stiff and prickly; borne on short, persistent pegs, they spread out and up to reveal the lower side of the shoot. Cones 100–180mm, red-brown, cigar-shaped; hang downwards from the shoots; cone-scales are square or irregularly notched at the tips. Forest tree in northern Europe and in mountains as far south as the Alps and Balkan Peninsula; widely planted for timber.

Pines

Sitka Spruce *Picea sitchensis* Up to 60m. Similar to Norway Spruce but the branches have stiff and slightly pendulous small side-shoots. Conical, evergreen tree, trunk stout, sometimes with buttresses. Bark grey, peeling in thin scales or plates. Main branches ascending or level. Needles 15–30mm, dark green above, with two conspicuous white bands beneath. Flattened, stiff and pointed, they are borne on persistent peg-like bases. Cones 60–100mm long, pendulous, bluntly cigar-shaped, with diamond-shaped, papery scales which are irregularly toothed at the tips. Native to North America but commonly planted for timber in north-west and central Europe.

White Spruce *Picea glauca* Up to 30m. An eyecatching, blue-white tree. The bruised foliage usually gives off a strong, unpleasant smell. Evergreen, narrowly conical but older trees become rounded. The branches turn up at the tips. Bark cracking into rounded plates. Needles 12–13mm, pale bluish-green; four-sided, stiff and bluntly tipped with peg-like bases, they spread out from the sides and top of the shoot. Cones 25–60mm, orange-brown, pendulous, cylindrical to shortly cigar-shaped with rounded scales. Native to North America and often planted as a timber tree in northern Europe.

Western Hemlock-spruce
Tsuga heterophylla Up to 70m.
Narrow and graceful, this
evergreen has pendulous
young shoots and a sharply
nodding leader. Bark grey,
becoming purple-brown and
flaking. Young shoots have
long, light brown hairs and
prominent cushion-like bases
which persist after the needles
fall. Needles 6–20mm, dark
green above with two broad
white bands beneath; blunt,
hard and flattened they spread
out on either side of the
shoot. Cones 20–25mm,
pendulous, oval to cylindrical
with a few, rounded scales;
purplish, ripening brown.
Native to North America,
sometimes planted for timber
in north-west Europe.

Douglas-fir *Pseudotsuga menziesii*
Up to 100m. A tall evergreen
with resinous, aromatic
foliage. Conical tree, usually
less than maximum height in
Europe, with irregularly
whorled branches. Bark grey,
smooth eventually becoming
purplish-brown, ridged.
Shoots hairy. Needles 20–
35mm, dark green and grooved
above, with two white bands
beneath; very narrow, soft
with sharp points, they mostly
spread out to either side of
the shoot. Cones 50–100mm,
pendulous, oval; red or green
ripening brown; prominent
three-pointed bract beneath
each rounded scale. Native to
North America; widely grown
for timber, especially in
northern and central Europe.

31

Pines

Shore Pine *Pinus contorta* Up to 30m. Short, contorted branches form the bushy crown of this evergreen, which is often much smaller than its maximum height; young trees are bushy, older ones tall and narrow. Bark brown, cracking into corky squares. Needles 30–70mm x *c* 1mm, twisted and sharply pointed; borne in pairs. Cones 20–60mm, dark red when young, ripening to pale shiny brown in the second year; symmetrically oval, they form clusters of 2–4; cone-scales are tipped with a slender, fragile spike. Native to pacific North America, widely planted for timber on poor soils in north-west and central Europe.

Maritime Pine *Pinus pinaster* Up to 40m. Long and bare, the trunk of this evergreen tree supports an open crown of wide-spread branches bearing very long, stiff needles. Bark red-brown, deeply fissured. Twigs reddish-brown. Pairs of needles, 100–250mm x 2mm, are greyish-green. Cones 80–220mm, symmetrically conical to oval, in clusters of 3–5 at tips of shoots; pink ripening to pale, shiny brown in second year, persisting on tree; cone-scales have exposed end rhomboidal and keeled with prickly point. On light and sandy soils near the sea around the Mediterranean; planted elsewhere for timber and shelter.

Austrian Pine *Pinus nigra* Up to 50m. Very dense, rough foliage gives a dark overall appearance to this evergreen tree. Young specimens are pyramidal, old ones flat-topped. Bark grey-brown to black, very rough. Twigs yellowish-brown, rough with persistent leaf-bases. Needles 100–150mm long, in pairs grouped in whorls on twigs; stiff, toothed and thickened at the tips. Cones 50–80mm, usually in pairs; ripen in second year from pink to pale, shiny brown; the spreading scales have exposed ends keeled and spine-tipped. Found on alkaline and neutral soils in central Europe and coasts of southern Europe; also widely planted.

Scots Pine *Pinus sylvestris* 25–35m. Evergreen tree with reddish upper bark and a small, flat, often lop-sided crown. Young trees conical with whorled branches, older trees with long, bare trunks, branching only at top. Bark fissured, lighter and papery at top. Needles 25–80mm, paired, grey or bluish-green; twisted and finely toothed. Cones 20–80mm, in clusters of 1–3, oval-conical; ripen from pinkish-purple to dull grey-brown in second year; cone-scales have exposed ends flat or slightly pyramidal with a short spine. Seeds have a wing 15mm long. Forms forests on poor, light soils on high ground throughout Europe.

Pines

Dwarf Mountain Pine *Pinus mugo* Up to 10m. This shrubby upland pine hugs the ground, seldom reaching its maximum height although it can form a small conical tree. Evergreen, with numerous crooked, spreading stems and branches. Paired needles 30-80mm x 1.5-2mm, bright green, stiff and curved. Cones 20-50mm, in clusters of 1-3; oval; shiny brown, ripening in second year; exposed end of each scale usually flat with a central boss bearing a small spine. Native to high mountains of central Europe and the Balkan Peninsula; often planted in northern Europe as a sand-binder and as a wind- or avalanche-break elsewhere.

Aleppo Pine *Pinus halepensis* Up to 20m. Sparse but very bright, shiny green foliage clothes the branches of this evergreen tree. Trunk stout and, like branches, often twisted. Bark pale grey, becoming reddish-brown, fissured and flaking. Needles 60-150mm x 0.7mm, clear green; stiff, curved and spiny tipped; borne in pairs. Cones 50-120mm, shiny, reddish-brown; borne on thick, scaly, recurved stalks; ripen in second year; cone-scales convex at exposed ends. Seeds have a wing *c* 20mm long. Drought-resistant, common in hot, dry parts of the Mediterranean; often planted as a wind-break and soil stabiliser.

Stone Pine *Pinus pinea* Up to
30m. Radiating branches and a
flat crown give this stout pine
a distinctive umbrella-shape.
Evergreen tree with bare
trunk. Bark deeply fissured
and flaking to reveal reddish-
orange patches. Twigs
greyish-green, eventually
brown. Needles 100–200mm x
1.5–2mm, paired, slightly
twisted. Cones 80–140mm,
ripening from yellowish-green
to shiny brown over three
years. The exposed end
of each scale is weakly
pyramidal. Seeds have a wing
less than 1mm long. Found on
light soils all around the
Mediterranean coasts, planted
both for ornament and for the
edible seeds.

Arolla Pine *Pinus cembra* 25–
40m. This densely foliaged
pine retains its branches, even
the lowest ones, so that the
trunk is almost completely
hidden. Evergreen tree with
short, level branches. Bark
scaly, marked with resin
blisters. Twigs covered with
brownish-orange hair.
Needles 50–80mm x 1mm, shiny
green; stiff, grouped in erect
bundles of 5 crowded on
twigs. Cones 50–80mm oval
and short-stalked, ripening
from bluish to purplish-brown
over 3 years; cone-scales are
rounded, thickened at tip and
minutely hairy. Seeds
wingless. A mountain species
native to the Alps and
Carpathians; planted for
timber in parts of northern
Europe.

Pines/Willows

Weymouth Pine *Pinus strobus*
Up to 50m. Has dense,
horizontally held needles with
distinctive tufts of hairs at the
bases. Evergreen tree,
eventually broadly pyramidal
in outline. Bark of mature
trees brown and fissured.
Young shoots have tufts of
reddish-brown down below
the needle bundles. Flexible
needles 50–140mm, bluish-
green; arranged in bundles of
5. Sticky cones, 80–200mm, are
large, pendulous and
cylindrical, but often curve
towards the tip; ripen in
second year. Seeds have a
wing 18–25mm wide. North
American species formerly
widely planted for timber, but
susceptible to blister rust and
less common nowadays.

Bay Willow *Salix pentandra* 5–
7m. Highly glossed leaves and
shiny twigs give a varnished
appearance to this small tree
or tall shrub. Branches
spreading, with reddish-
brown twigs. Leaves 50–
120mm, elliptical to lance-
shaped, long-pointed,
leathery, dark and very shiny
above, paler below; yellow
glands tip the minute
marginal teeth. Hairy-stalked
catkins appear with the leaves
May–June; the dense,
cylindrical males, 20–50mm,
are pale yellow and borne on
separate trees from the
shorter, greenish females.
Seeds silky plumed. Common
along waterways and in wet
soils in most of Europe except
the Mediterranean islands.

Crack Willow *Salix fragilis* Up to 25m. Frequently pollarded, its short, thick trunks often lean over rivers and streams. Crown broad, rounded. Twigs smooth, olive-brown; very brittle where they join the branches. Leaves 90–150mm, dark shiny green above, bluish-grey beneath; long-pointed, lance-shaped; margins have coarse, gland-tipped teeth. Male catkins yellow, females green, each 40–60mm, borne on short, hairy stalks but on separate trees, appearing with the leaves April–May. Found on deep, wet, lowland soils, often planted on the fringes of farmland. Occurring throughout most of Europe but patchily distributed in the Mediterranean region.

White Willow *Salix alba* 10–25m. A distinctive silvery grey when seen from a distance, this tree has upswept branches forming a narrow crown. Hairy twigs become smooth and olive to brown. Leaves 50–100mm, narrow, pointed and minutely toothed; covered with silky silvery hairs but the upper surface eventually becomes dull green and naked. Catkins on densely hairy stalks appear with the leaves April–May, males and females on separate trees; pale yellow, erect males 40–50mm, greenish females shorter and more slender. Widespread throughout Europe, usually growing by running water.

Willows

Golden Weeping Willow *Salix* x *sepulcralis* Up to 12m. A luxuriant leafy dome, this willow has a curtain of weeping branches, the tips sometimes reaching to the ground. Twigs golden-yellow, hairy but becoming smooth. Leaves 70–120mm, finely toothed, narrowly lance-shaped and pointed; initially hairy but become smooth, bright green above, bluish below. Catkins 30–40mm, borne on shaggily hairy stalks, appear with leaves in April; narrowly cylindrical, often curved. Trees are usually male. Of hybrid origin, widely planted for ornament. Its parent Weeping Willow (*S. babylonica*) has smooth twigs and shorter, stalkless catkins.

Grey Sallow *Salix cinerea* subsp. *cinerea* Up to 10m. Both leaves and twigs of this small tree or tall shrub are felted with grey hairs. Crown broad. Leaves 20–160mm, rather variable but have toothed, inrolled margins and may have two ear-shaped stipules at base of leaf stalk; hairy or shiny above, they are grey felted below. Male and female catkins 20–30mm, stalkless, appear on separate trees in March–April, before the leaves; erect, cylindrical to oval, they are densely grey-hairy with darker flecks. Common in wet fenland and marshes in most of Europe, except Iberia and some Mediterranean islands.

Goat Willow *Salix caprea* Up to
10m. The soft, furry catkins
are known as 'pussy willows'.
Small tree or tall shrub with
open, spreading crown. Twigs
thick and stiff; smooth and
yellowish-brown. Leaves 50–
120mm, broadly oval to elliptic,
shortly pointed; dull green
above, grey-woolly below,
margins with irregular, gland-
tipped teeth; stalk sometimes
has two small ear-shaped
stipules at base. Male and
female catkins 15–25mm, borne
on separate trees March–
April, appearing before leaves;
they are erect, ovoid, stalkless
and silky silver-grey. Grows
along hedgerows and edges of
woods, often in quite dry
places, throughout Europe.

Osier *Salix viminalis* 3–6m.
Frequent cropping provides a
'head' of long, straight, pliant
twigs. Small tree or tall shrub.
Twigs densely grey-hairy at
first, later shiny olive or
brown. Leaves 100–150mm,
dull green above, densely
silvery-silky below; they are
narrow and tapering with
inrolled margins. Male and
female catkins 15–30mm, borne
on separate trees, appear with
the leaves in February–April;
crowded at end of twigs, they
are erect or curved and
densely hairy; males yellow,
females brownish. Common
throughout lowland Europe
but mainly planted (for the
twigs or withies) or a relict of
cultivation in the West.

Willows

White Poplar *Populus alba* Up to 20m, rarely to 40m. Tall, often leaning in the soft ground it favours, this tree has a very pale crown. Spreading tree, suckering at base. Young twigs densely white-hairy. Leaves 30–90mm, irregularly lobed, those near twig tips deeply three- to five-lobed, like a maple; dark green above, pure white on hairy underside; stalks round. Hairy catkins appear February–March, before the leaves; males 40–70mm with purple anthers; smaller females, on separate trees, have greenish stigmas. A widespread native from central to south-east Europe but ornamental and introduced to many areas.

Aspen *Populus tremula* Up to 20m. Fluttering in the slightest breeze, the leaves of this slender tree have their movements accentuated by the flashing of the pale undersides. Freely suckering, with thinly hairy young twigs. Leaves 15–80mm, broadly oval to almost circular, bluntly and coarsely toothed; dark green above but very pale beneath. Leaf stalk is flattened from side to side, enabling leaf to twist easily. Catkins 50–80mm, appear February–March on separate trees; males have reddish-purple anthers, females have pink stigmas. A short-lived tree, common on poor soils throughout Europe, often forming groves.

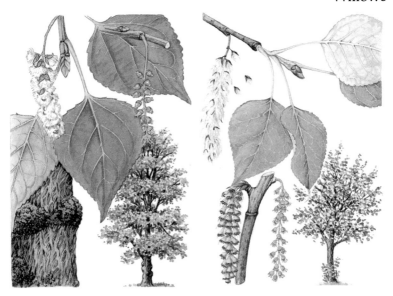

Black Poplar *Populus nigra* Up to 35m. Best known as a very tall, straight and narrow cultivated form (Lombardy Poplar, var. *italica*), the common wild tree is broad and rounded with burrs and large rough swellings on the trunk. Twigs smooth, shiny orange-brown. Leaves 50–100mm, rhombic to triangular-oval with fine, blunt teeth on margins; lower surface only slightly paler than upper; leaf stalk flattened from side to side. Loose catkins appear March–April, before the leaves, males with crimson anthers, females with greenish stigmas, on separate trees; initially 30–50mm, longer in fruit. Widespread in central and southern Europe.

Balm-of-Gilead *Populus candicans* Up to 25m. Broad spreading tree, giving off a strong balsam scent, especially on wet spring days as the buds break. Suckering tree with grey-green bark. Young twigs fragrant, thinly hairy, soon becoming glossy brown. Leaves 50–150mm, fragrant, heart-shaped with fine, blunt and hairy teeth. Leaf stalk slightly flattened on upper and lower sides, with two glands near the top. Catkins appear in March, just before leaves. Only females are known; 40–60mm long in flower, they reach 160mm before releasing silky hairy seeds. Native to North America; commonly planted in Europe, often naturalised.

Walnuts

Walnut *Juglans regia* Up to 30m. Wide-spreading tree with a thick trunk and leathery, aromatic leaves. Bark grey, smooth. Twigs marked with distinctive Y-shaped scars where leaves have fallen. Leaves pinnately divided into 7-9 entire leaflets each 60-150mm, those towards leaf tips larger than the others. Flowers May–June; males in solitary, pendulous catkins of 50-150mm, on new growth, females in clusters of 2-5 on old wood. Fruit 40-50mm, contains an oval, wrinkled stone, the familiar walnut of commerce. Native to the Balkans and parts of Asia, but planted and naturalised since ancient times in many parts of Europe.

Black Walnut *Juglans nigra* Up to 50m. Large, fast-growing tree similar to Common Walnut but with finer, more abundant, foliage. Bark black or brown, deeply fissured into diamond-shaped ridges. Leaves pinnately divided into 15-23 leaflets, each 60-120mm long, oval to lance-shaped, pointed and irregularly fine-toothed; they are hairy beneath. Flowers May–June with male catkins of 50-150mm and female flowers in clusters of 5. Fruit 35-50mm, green and hairy, containing an oval, ridged stone. A native of North America, widely planted for timber in eastern parts of central Europe.

Silver Birch *Betula pendula* Up
to 30m. Slender, elegant tree
with distinctive, silvery-white
bark broken into dark,
rectangular plates at the base
of the trunk. Branches
pendulous towards tips.
Young twigs warty with pale
resin-glands. Leaves usually
25–50mm, oval to triangular,
base cut straight across or
slightly heart-shaped; sharply
and unevenly double-toothed
margins. Flowers April–May.
Terminal male catkins 30–
60mm, axillary females only
15–35mm, made up of scales
with down-curved lobes and
female flowers. Short-lived
pioneer species on light, sandy
soils. Found throughout much
of Europe, but absent, or
confined to mountains, in
south.

Downy Birch *Betula pubescens*
Up to 25m. Small tree or often
a shrub, especially in arctic
regions. Bark brown or grey
and smooth. Branches
spreading. Young twigs
covered with downy, white
hairs. Oval leaves up to 55mm,
rounded or triangular at the
base, with regular, coarsely
toothed margins. Flowers
April–May; terminal male
catkins 30–60mm; axillary
females 10–40mm, composed of
scales with spreading or
upswept lateral lobes and
female flowers. Short-lived,
growing mainly on wet soils.
Cold-tolerant, common
throughout northern and
central Europe, only on
mountains in south.

Birches

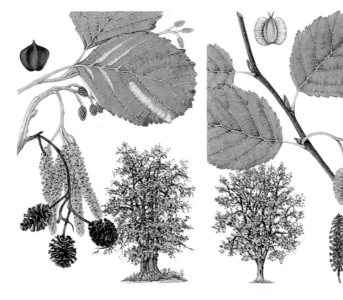

Common Alder *Alnus glutinosa* Up to 20m. In winter the old cones are conspicuous on the bare twigs. Small, broadly conical tree. Young twigs sticky and covered with orange warts. Winter buds are stalked. Leaves 40-100mm, bright green; round or widest above the middle, doubly toothed, tip often shallowly notched. Flowers February–March, before the leaves. Pendulous male catkins 20-60mm, initially purple, later yellowish; females 15mm, grouped in stalked clusters of 3-8, purplish becoming green. Fruit 10-30mm, woody, resembles a small cone containing narrowly winged nutlets. Common throughout most of Europe, especially in wet places and beside water.

Green Alder *Alnus viridis* Up to 5m. Resembling a small Common Alder, this close relative grows in mountainous areas. Twigs smooth or minutely hairy. Winter buds without stalks. Leaves 40-90mm elliptical to roughly circular with sharply double-toothed margins; sticky when young. Flowers in April appear with the leaves. Male catkins 50-120mm, yellow; females 10mm, in clusters of 3-5 with several leaves at base of stalk, initially green, later reddish. Fruit 15mm, woody, cone-like; contains broadly winged nutlets. A mountain species of central and eastern Europe but extending to France and Corsica and north to Sweden.

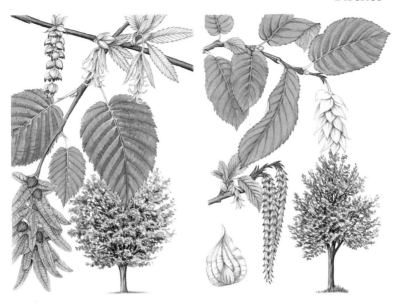

Hornbeam *Carpinus betulus* Up to 30m. Rather gnarled and contorted, Hornbeams are often coppiced or pollarded. Trunk and branches frequently twisted or fluted; twigs thickly hairy. Bark pale grey, smooth, sometimes fissured. Leaves 40–100mm, oval, sharply pointed, rounded at base; sharply double-toothed margins; underside has c 15 pairs of hairy, parallel veins. Flowers April–May; pendulous yellow male catkins up to 50mm; green females 20mm, reaching 50–140mm in fruit. Each pair of nuts is attached to a leaf-like, three-lobed involucre up to 40mm long. Common hedgerow and woodland species, especially in coppices. Found throughout Europe.

Hop-hornbeam *Ostrya carpinifolia* Up to 12m. Small slender tree with pale, papery fruiting heads resembling clusters of hops. Bark brown; cracks and peels. Twigs hairy with orange warts. Leaves 50–80mm, oval, long-pointed, sharply double-toothed; 12–15 pairs of veins. Flowers in April, with the leaves; pendulous yellow male catkins up to 100mm long; females much shorter, in fruit 30–50mm long, dense and roughly cylindrical, composed of many pale green or whitish, leaf-like involucres, each enclosing a single nut. Grows in hilly woodland fringes and scrub in southern Europe from France and Corsica eastwards.

Hazel *Corylus avellana* Up to 12m. Bushy tree or shrub with wrinkled, bristly leaves and nuts seated in ragged cups. Twigs have reddish, glandular hairs. Leaves 100mm, with sharp, double-toothed margins. Flowers January–April, catkins appearing before leaves; male catkins up to 80mm, pendulous, bright yellow, in clusters of 1–4; spike-like females, 5mm, have bright red styles. Hard-shelled nut 5–20mm, enveloped within a ragged, leafy, cup-like involucre about as long as the nut; edible kernel is the familiar hazelnut. Common in hedges and woods, especially as an undershrub, often coppiced. Found throughout Europe.

Beech *Fagus sylvatica* Up to 40m. Forming dense-canopied woods, beeches create a deep litter of decay-resistant dark-brown leaves which discourages ground plants. Broad tree with smooth grey bark. Leaves 40–90mm, oval to elliptical with wavy margins and 7–8 pairs of parallel veins. Flowers, April–May, are yellowish; males in drooping, long-stalked heads, paired females surrounded by a stalked, spiny four-lobed involucre which in fruit reaches 20–50mm and contains two triangular, brown nuts. Common throughout western and central Europe on well-drained soils, especially chalk and limestone; often planted for timber and ornament.

Sweet Chestnut *Castanea sativa*
Up to 30m. In summer the
clusters of erect catkins of this
tree are visible from some
distance. Bark greyish, often
spirally fissured. Leaves 100–
250mm with sharp teeth on
margins. Flowers June–July;
slender, catkins with
numerous yellowish male
flowers in the upper part and
female flowers grouped in
threes towards the base. Each
female cluster is surrounded
by a green, spiny cupule
which forms the outer husk of
the fruit, containing 1–3 shiny,
reddish-brown edible nuts.
Found mainly on well-drained,
acid or neutral soils. Native to
southern Europe, widely
planted and naturalised
elsewhere.

Red Oak *Quercus rubra* Up to
35m. With leaves turning
scarlet or deep blood-red, this
oak produces an outstanding
display of autumn colour.
Broadly domed tree with
stout, dark red twigs. Matt
leaves 120–220mm, divided
about halfway to midrib into
several lobes each with 1–3
slender teeth; grey underside
has a few hairs in vein axils.
Flowers May, males in catkins,
females in clusters. Acorns
ripen in second year; acorn
cup 18–25mm diameter, very
shallow, the closely pressed,
oval scales thin and finely
hairy. Native to eastern North
America and one of several
species widely planted in
Europe for ornament.

Oaks

Kermes Oak *Quercus coccifera*
Up to 5m. Closely resembling a holly bush, this small evergreen tree or low shrub has stiff and spiny leaves. Young twigs yellowish, with star-shaped hairs. Leaves 15–40mm, oval to oblong, sometimes heart-shaped at the base, with wavy and spine-toothed margins. Leaf stalk only 1-4mm long. Flowers April–May, males in catkins, females in clusters. Acorns ripen in second year; shallow acorn cups have stiff, more or less spiny and spreading scales. Widespread throughout the Mediterranean, especially in the hotter, drier parts, though, curiously, absent from much of Italy.

Evergreen Oak *Quercus ilex* Up to 25m. Like its small relative, the Kermes Oak, this tree is evergreen but with less stiff and spiny foliage. Twigs grey-brown, hairy. Leaves 30–70mm, thick and leathery, white-felted beneath. In young trees leaves often entire but in older ones have wavy margins with short spiny teeth. Flowers June, males in catkins, females in clusters of 1-5. Acorns ripen in same year; cup of 12mm diameter with close-pressed, felted scales encloses one-third to half the acorn. Native to the Mediterranean; widely planted ornamental elsewhere, sometimes naturalised in western and southern Europe.

Cork Oak *Quercus suber* Up to 20m. Evergreen tree often seen with the lower part of the trunk peeled of the thick outer bark, which yields cork, revealing bright orange inner bark. Leaves 30–70mm, dark green above, white-hairy below, oblong-oval with wavy and toothed margins. Flowers May–June, males in catkins, females in clusters. Acorns of early flowering trees ripen in same year, those of late flowering trees in second year; cup 12–18mm diameter, long, spreading scales in upper half, close-pressed scales in lower; half encloses acorn. Common in southern Europe, often planted for commercial cork.

Turkey Oak *Quercus cerris* Up to 35m. Large, spreading oak, with a dull, sombre appearance. Twigs rough, brown or grey and shortly hairy. Rather variable leaves, usually 50–100mm, with 4–7 pairs of narrow lobes; rough and dull above, they are woolly below. Flowers May–June, males in catkins, females in clusters of 1–5. Acorns ripen in the second year; half to two-thirds enclosed in woody cups 15–22mm diameter. Thick, pointed scales curve outwards from the cup. Native to southern half of Europe except Spain and Portugal, and widely introduced elsewhere.

Oaks

Sessile Oak *Quercus petraea* Up to 40m. Similar to Pedunculate Oak with which it often dominates in woods, this domed tree has hairier leaves and stalkless acorns. Trunk long and smooth. Bark purplish-grey. Leaves 70–120mm, with 5–8 pairs of rounded lobes; pale undersides have fine, close-pressed hairs, plus reddish tufts in the vein axils. Flowers May, males in catkins, females in clusters. Acorns in clusters of up to 6 ripen in same year. Cups 12–18mm diameter, shallow, stalkless, with thin, downy scales. Common on light soils. Widespread throughout Europe except for parts of the Mediterranean.

Pedunculate Oak *Quercus robur* Up to 45m. Massive, spreading tree, often dominating woodland; many individuals are very long-lived. Young twigs brownish, hairy. Leaves 100–120mm, 5–7 pairs of lobes plus small ear-shaped projections at the base and a stalk not more than 5mm long. Flowers May–June, males in catkins, females in clusters. Acorns ripen the same year, forming clusters of 1–5 on a stalk 40–80mm long. The scales of the shallow, 11–18mm diameter cups are fused together except for their tips. Frequently a dominant woodland tree on heavy, alkaline soils. Common in most of Europe.

Downy Oak *Quercus pubescens*
Up to 25m. A grey-leaved oak
found in dry, hilly regions.
Small tree or even a shrub,
but capable of reaching
moderate size. Twigs densely
grey-hairy. Leaves 40-120mm
have shallower, more
forward-pointing lobes than
in other deciduous oaks; grey
velvety undersides of young
leaves gradually become
smooth. Flowers May, males
in catkins, females in clusters
of 1-3. Acorns ripen in the
same year; stalkless, shallow
cups of 15mm diameter have
close-pressed and grey-woolly
scales. Grows in dry limestone
hills in south-central and
western Europe.

Wych Elm *Ulmus glabra* Up to
40m. Broad, spreading tree
with stout, stiffly hairy young
twigs. Leaves 100-180mm,
rounded to elliptical and long-
pointed; stiffly hairy above,
softer-haired beneath; veins in
10-18 pairs. Leaf base
asymmetric, one side curved
to overlap and conceal the leaf
stalk. Flower clusters appear
February–March, before the
leaves; purplish-red; perianth
has 4-5 lobes. Fruit 15-20mm;
seed centrally placed in the
papery wing. Found on rich,
damp soils in hilly areas,
especially by water. Native to
most of Europe but absent
from Mediterranean islands.
Somewhat resistant to Dutch
elm disease.

Elms

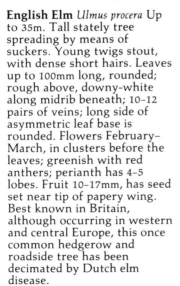

English Elm *Ulmus procera* Up to 35m. Tall stately tree spreading by means of suckers. Young twigs stout, with dense short hairs. Leaves up to 100mm long, rounded; rough above, downy-white along midrib beneath; 10-12 pairs of veins; long side of asymmetric leaf base is rounded. Flowers February–March, in clusters before the leaves; greenish with red anthers; perianth has 4-5 lobes. Fruit 10-17mm, has seed set near tip of papery wing. Best known in Britain, although occurring in western and central Europe, this once common hedgerow and roadside tree has been decimated by Dutch elm disease.

Smooth-leaved Elm *Ulmus carpinifolia* Up to 30m. One of several related and very similar elms. Narrow tree with long, pendulous and smooth young twigs. Suckers often present. Leaves 60–80mm, pointed, widest above the middle and smooth on both sides; 12 pairs of veins; long side of asymmetric leaf base makes 90° turn to join stalk. Small flowers open in March, in clusters, before the leaves; anthers red; perianth has 4-5 lobes. Fruit 7-18mm; seed set near top of papery wing. Prefers deep, moist soils along roadsides and hedgerows. Native to most of Europe except Scandinavia; widely planted.

European White Elm *Ulmus laevis* Up to 35m. Clusters of long-stalked flowers flutter in spring on the bare twigs of this tall, open tree. Crown wide-spreading. Bark, initially smooth becomes deeply ridged with age. Leaves 60-130mm, oval to nearly round; usually smooth above but downy grey beneath, with 12-19 pairs of veins and a very asymmetric leaf base. Flowers appear in March in clusters, before the leaves, reddish; 4-5 perianth lobes. Fruits 10-12mm, pendulous with fringe of white hairs on papery wing. Native to central and south-eastern Europe, mainly in river valleys; occasionally planted for shelter elsewhere.

Southern Nettle-tree *Celtis australis* Up to 25m. Leaves of this tree resemble those of the nettle, but do not sting. They are 40-150mm, narrowly oval and sharply toothed, tapering to the often twisted tip; upper surface stiffly hairy, lower downy-white, especially on the veins. Flowers appear with young leaves in May; solitary in leaf axils; dull brownish-green, with 4-5 perianth lobes. Berry-like fruit *c* 10mm, fleshy and edible; long-stalked; ripens from brownish-red to black. Native to southern Europe, especially central region from Italy to Yugoslavia; also planted elsewhere as a street tree and ornamental.

Mulberries

Black Mulberry *Morus nigra*
Up to 12m. Bushy-headed tree
with fruits resembling outsize
raspberries. Trunk short and
often leaning, supporting
thick, twisted branches. Bark,
orange-brown cracking and
shredding. Young twigs exude
milky latex when cut. Leaves
60–200mm, heart-shaped,
toothed or lobed; rough
above, softly hairy beneath.
Flowers May, in catkin-like
spikes, males 25mm long,
females about half this length.
Fruit 20–25mm, soft and
fleshy; dark red or purplish;
very tart and acid-tasting until
fully ripe. Originating in
central Asia but cultivated for
centuries in Europe as a fruit
tree, and now widely
naturalised.

Fig *Ficus carica* Up to 8m. Large,
long-stalked leaves and unique
fruits make this low, wide-
spreading tree difficult to
confuse with any other.
Leaves 100–200mm long and
broad, thick and leathery;
palmately divided into 3–5
rounded lobes; sparsely
bristly, rough to touch.
Flowers borne on inside of a
hollow, fleshy and swollen,
pear-shaped structure which
ripens in second year; when
fully developed fruit is 50–
80mm long and brownish or
violet-green. Native to south-
west Asia and possibly to the
Mediterranean where it is
widely grown for fruit and
shade; sometimes grown for
ornament in northern Europe.

Tulip-tree *Liriodendron tulipifera*
Up to 45m. The distinctively
shaped leaves of this tall tree
are light and flutter like those
of poplars. Slender, straight-
sided young crown becomes
domed with age. Leaves 70–
120mm, have 1, 2 or rarely 3
lobes on each side; bright
green above, slightly bluish
and waxy beneath, turning
butter-yellow in autumn.
Flowers May–June, cup-
shaped, resembling yellow-
green tulips; 9 perianth-
segments *c* 50mm long, inner 6
with an orange band near
base. Fruit 50–85mm, narrow
and cone-like. Native to North
America; widely planted in
Europe for ornament and
timber.

Evergreen Magnolia *Magnolia
grandiflora* Up to 30m. Creamy-
white flowers of this
spreading evergreen tree are
very large and conspicuous.
Large branches make a conical
crown. Leaves 80–160mm,
entire, thick and leathery;
very shiny on upper surface
but covered with rusty hairs
beneath. Flowers July–
November; blooms up to
250mm diameter, 6 petal-like
segments; initially conical,
gradually opening almost flat.
Fruit forms a cone-like
structure 50–60mm long.
Native to eastern North
America; widely grown in
Europe as an ornamental.
Several other magnolias,
especially hardy deciduous
species, are also commonly
grown.

Laurels/Planes

Sweet Bay *Laurus nobilis* Up to 20m. Bushy, densely branched evergreen with leaves giving a strong, aromatic scent when bruised. Leaves 50–100mm, lance-shaped with wavy margins and dotted with numerous, tiny translucent oil glands. The short leaf stalk is dark red. Flowers are borne April–June in small clusters on separate male and female trees; yellow; 4-petalled. Berries 10–15mm, oval; green, turning black when fully ripe. Native to dry areas of the Mediterranean. Widely cultivated as a pot-herb in Europe, often grown as a clipped shrub.

London Plane *Platanus* x *hispanica* Up to 35m. The thin grey bark of this broad, spreading tree regularly flakes away to reveal a mosaic of large buff and yellow patches. Leaves up to 250mm x 250mm, palmately divided into 5 triangular lobes with forward-pointing teeth. Flowers June, heads globose, in strings; males in 2–6 yellowish-green heads, females in 2–5 crimson heads. Seed-heads 25mm, brown; remain on tree until following spring before breaking up to release abundant, white-haired seeds. Of hybrid or perhaps cultivated origin, vigorous and pollution tolerant; one of the most common street trees in Europe.

Quince *Cydonia oblonga* Up to 7.5m. Small tree or shrub resembling an apple tree but for the larger, solitary flowers and very hard, sweet-smelling fruit. Young shoots are woolly but become smooth. Leaves 50–100mm, oval, entire and woolly-grey below. Flowers in May are solitary, 40–45mm, pink or white, with short hairy stalks; 5 petals, cup-shaped. Fruit only 25–35mm in wild plants but reaches 120mm in cultivated ones; globose or pear-shaped; flesh yellow, very woody. Native to Asia but cultivated in much of Europe and naturalised in places, especially in the south.

Common Pear *Pyrus communis* Up to 20m. The leaves of this narrow tree turn yellow to dark red in autumn. Young twigs reddish-brown, usually thorny in older trees. Leaves 50–80mm, pointed, oval to elliptical, sharply and finely toothed on margins; densely hairy when unfurling, but soon smooth. Flowers April, in clusters appearing with leaves; 5 petals 12–14mm, white; anthers reddish-purple. Fruit 60–160mm, pear-shaped to globose and yellowish to brown; flesh sweet or tart, gritty. Originating in western Asia, anciently introduced to Europe and widespread in woods and hedgerows. The cultivated pear (var. *culta*) has sweet fruit.

Roses

Crab Apple *Malus sylvestris* 2–10m. Spiny wild trees have white flowers, the unarmed descendants of domesticated trees have pink-tinged flowers. Small spreading tree with large, twisted branches and dense foliage. Leaves 80–110mm, toothed, oval, elliptical or almost orbicular and smooth on both surfaces when mature. Flowers May–June, appearing with the leaves; 5 petals; 30–40mm diameter, white or pinkish. Fruit 25–30mm, smaller than that of cultivated apple; yellow-green flushed with red; hard and sour. Native to chalky, hilly regions in much of Europe; anciently domesticated, no longer used as a fruit tree but widely naturalised.

Cultivated Apple *Malus domestica* Up to 15m. Similar to Crab Apple but instantly recognisable by the large fruits which are heavy enough to weigh down the branches. Small tree with downy twigs. Leaves 40–130mm, oval-elliptical, pointed and slightly toothed; sparsely hairy above and more densely woolly below. Flowers May–June, appearing with the leaves, 30–40mm diameter; 5 petals, usually pink but occasionally white. Firm, sweet-tasting fruit, exceeding 50mm, varies in colour from green to red or brown. Of hybrid origin and divided into thousands of cultivars, it is the best known orchard tree in Europe; often escapes and becomes naturalised.

True Service-tree *Sorbus domestica* Up to 20m. Resembling tiny hard pears, the astringent fruits of this tree become edible only after being frosted. Branches spreading to horizontal. Bark shredding. Leaves pinnately divided into 6–8 pairs of oblong leaflets; each leaflet 30–55mm long, blade symmetrical at base, toothed towards top and softly hairy beneath, mainly on veins. Flowers May in domed clusters, each flower 16–18mm diameter, with 5 petals and 5 styles. Fruit 20mm or more long, pear-shaped, green or brownish. Mainly in dry, deciduous woods. Native to southern Europe and the Mediterranean region; often naturalised elsewhere.

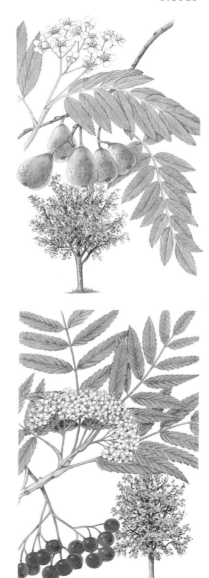

Rowan *Sorbus aucuparia* 5–20m. A deep, extensive root system allows this bushy tree to cling to exposed rocks and mountain sides. Crown rounded and open with erect to spreading branches. Leaves pinnately divided into 5–10 pairs of oblong leaflets, each 30–60mm long with blade toothed in upper part, asymmetric at base and grey-hairy below. Flower clusters in May, each 5-petalled flower 8–10mm diameter, with 3–4 styles. Fruit 6–9mm, globose or oval, scarlet. In woods or open places in most conditions except on waterlogged soils; common on high ground. Native to most of Europe frequently seen as a street tree.

Roses

Wild Service-tree *Sorbus torminalis* Up to 25m. Leaves like those of the Plane tree and brown fruits distinguish this from other species of *Sorbus*. Domed tree, sometimes only a large, spreading shrub. Leaves 50–100mm, dark green, hairy beneath when young but almost smooth when mature; the lowest of the 3–5 pairs of toothed and pointed lobes spread horizontally. Flower clusters May–June; flowers 10–15mm diameter; 5 petals, 2 styles. Fruit 120–180mm, brown, fleshy and dotted with numerous warts. Scattered but widespread in deciduous woods, usually on clay soils. Native to all but the far north of Europe.

Whitebeam *Sorbus aria* Up to 25m. Pallid green from a distance, this tree stands out in spring when the white undersides of the leaves are most noticeable. Leaves 50–120mm, oval with irregular teeth curving towards rounded tips; bright green above, white felted beneath; 10–14 pairs of veins. Flower clusters May–June; each 5-petalled flower 10–15mm diameter. Ovoid fruit 8–15mm, scarlet with many small warts. Native to woods and rocky places in most of Europe, mainly on limestone; confined to mountains in the south. One form with yellow-flecked fruits, and another with silvery leaves, are common street trees.

Swedish Whitebeam *Sorbus intermedia* Up to 15m. Rather squat and rounded, this tree has a short trunk and domed crown. Leaves 60–120mm, 7–9 pairs of veins; glossy green, felted beneath with yellowish-grey hairs; lobes near base of blade reach one-third of the way to midrib, those towards tip are progressively shallower, eventually reduced to coarse teeth. Flower clusters in May; white, 5 petalled flowers 12–20mm diameter. Fruits 12–15mm, oblong-ovoid, scarlet with a few warts. Native to Scandinavia and the regions around the Baltic; tolerant of air pollution, commonly used as a street tree.

Loquat *Eriobotrya japonica* Up to 10m. A dense velvet of rusty hairs covers the twigs and undersides of the leaves of this evergreen tree or shrub. Leaves 100–250mm, strongly veined, elliptic-oblong or widest above the middle with toothed margins; dark, glossy green upper side contrasts strongly with red-brown underside. Fragrant flowers appear November–April in terminal clusters; *c* 10mm, 5 yellowish-white petals are often obscured by reddish hairs. Fruit 30–60mm, deep yellow; sweet and edible, resembling small apricot with a crown of persistent sepals. Native to China; widely cultivated in southern Europe as a fruit tree and ornamental.

Roses

Snowy Mespil *Amelanchier ovalis* Up to 5m. Young leaves add a touch of bronze to the drift of white blossom in spring. Slender tree or shrub with black bark. Young twigs white and woolly, becoming smooth with age. Leaves 25–50mm, may be oval or rounded and coarsely toothed or entire; white-woolly below. Starry white flowers with 5 narrow petals form erect, woolly clusters of 3–8. Fruit less than 10mm, berry-like, crowned with persistent sepals; ripens blue-black; edible. Native to southern and central Europe, in open woodland and rocky areas, mainly on limestone; often planted for ornament.

Medlar *Mespilus germanica* Up to 6m. Small tree or spreading shrub with fruits resembling large brown rose-hips. Young twigs densely covered with white hairs. Leaves 50–150mm, dull yellowish-green and crinkled; lance-shaped to inverted-oval, with distinctly sunken veins; may be entire or minutely toothed; felted with white hairs below. Flowers May–June, each white bloom 30–60mm diameter, solitary; narrow sepals longer than 5 broad petals. Fruit 20–30mm, dull brown, globose, with a depression surrounded by persistent sepals; edible when overripe. Native to moist, open woodlands of south-east Europe; widely naturalised in central and western areas.

Hawthorn *Crataegus monogyna*
Up to 18m. Usually cut back
and laid to form dense,
thorny, animal-proof hedges,
and only occasionally allowed
to reach its full height.
Thorns numerous, up to
15mm long. Shiny leaves 15–
45mm long, divided into 3–7
lobes reaching more than
halfway to the midrib; lobes
are entire or toothed near the
tip. Flowers May–September,
8–15mm diameter; 5 petals,
white to pale pink; each has a
single style. Fruit 7–14mm dark
or bright red; contains a single
seed. Very common in woods
and thickets as well as hedges,
especially on alkaline soils.
Native throughout Europe.

Midland Hawthorn *Crataegus
laevigata* Up to 10m. Shade
tolerant and less thorny than
its larger relative the
Hawthorn. Trunk fluted.
Thorns few, 6–15mm long.
Leaves 15–60mm, rather
leathery, with 3–5 lobes which
rarely reach halfway to the
midrib; lobes are toothed at
the base. Flowers May–June,
15–24mm, white; each has 5
petals and 2–3 styles. Fruit 6–
13mm, deep red; contains 2
seeds. Usually found in oak
woods on heavy, moist soils.
Native to central Europe as
far west as France and Britain.
Red, double-flowered forms
are common street trees.

Roses

Crataegus calycina Up to 11m. Elongated fruits most easily distinguish this woodland species of Hawthorn from its relatives. Thorns few, only 4–13mm long. Thin leaves 25–65mm long and broad; divided into toothed lobes which reach only one-third of the way to the midrib; lowest lobe is often deeper than the others. Flowers May–June, 120–200mm diameter; each flower has 5 petals and a single style. Fruit 9–15mm; dark or bright red, roughly cylindrical; contains a single seed. Native to deciduous and evergreen woods in north and central Europe and replaces Hawthorn in the more extreme climates.

Peach *Prunus persica* Up to 6m. In autumn large, globular, red-flushed fruits distinguish this bushy, straight-branched tree from the similar Almond. Leaves 50–150mm x 20–40mm, lance-shaped, finely toothed, folded lengthways into a V-shape. Flowers March–May, usually solitary, appearing as leaf-buds open; flower tube is as broad as long; 5 petals 10–20mm, deep pink, occasionally pale pink or white. Fruit 40–80mm, globular, yellow flushed with red and downy; sweet and juicy. Origin obscure, but possibly native to China; cultivated in Europe in orchards and gardens. The Nectarine (var. *nucipersica*) is a smooth-fruited cultivar of peach.

Almond *Prunus dulcis* Up to 8m. One of the first to flower in spring, this open-crowned tree has profuse pink or white blossom. Leaves 40–130mm x 10–40mm, finely toothed, folded lengthways to form a shallow V-shape. Flowers March–April, mostly in pairs, appearing before leaves; short, bell-shaped tube and 5 spreading, pale pink or rarely white petals of 15–25mm. Fruit 35–60mm, oblong-oval, flattened, grey-green, velvety; flesh thin; large pitted stone is the familiar almond nut. Probably native to Asia; cultivated for the seeds throughout southern Europe and as an ornamental in the north.

Apricot *Prunus armeniaca* 3–10m. This small, rounded tree has reddish twigs and young leaves. Branches twisted; twigs smooth. Leaves 50–100mm finely toothed, nearly circular with abruptly pointed tips and straight or heart-shaped bases; mature leaves are dull green above and greenish-yellow beneath. Leaf stalk red; usually has two glands near the top. Flowers March–April before the leaves; short-stalked, solitary or paired; hairy flower-tube is bell-shaped; 5 petals 10–15mm, white or pale pink. Fruit 40–80mm, round, yellow to orange and downy. Native to central Asia and China; widely grown in southern Europe.

Roses

Cherry Plum *Prunus cerasifera*
Up to 8m. Spreading easily by
means of suckers, this small
round-headed tree or shrub
readily forms thickets or
hedges. Slender branches
numerous. Young twigs
green, smooth and glossy.
Leaves 40–70mm, oblong-oval,
tapering at both ends with
small, rounded teeth; smooth
and glossy above, downy veins
beneath. Solitary flowers
appear March, before the
leaves; 5 petals 8–10mm, white
or sometimes pale pink. Fruit
35mm yellow or red; smooth
and globose. Native to the
Balkan Peninsula; widely
planted and naturalised
elsewhere. A red-leaved form
(var. *pissardii*) is common as a
garden and street tree.

Blackthorn *Prunus spinosa* Up to
6m. Black and thorny, the
branches of this small tree or
shrub are dense and wide-
spreading. Trunks produce
numerous suckers. Intricately
branched, thorny twigs are
downy when young. Leaves
20–45mm, toothed, widest
above or below the middle;
dull and smooth above, hairy
on veins beneath. Numerous
flowers are solitary, appear
March–April, well before the
leaves; 5 white petals 5–8mm.
Fruit 10–15mm, short-stalked;
bluish-black with greyish,
waxy bloom; very astringent.
Grows in hedges and thickets,
often forming these itself by
means of suckers. Native to
Europe, except in extreme
north.

Plum *Prunus domestica* Up to
10m. Thorny in the wild, this
tree is usually unarmed in
cultivation. Leaves 30–80mm,
toothed; dull and smooth
above, downy beneath.
Flowers March–May, in
clusters of 2–3 appearing with
the leaves; 5 petals 7–12mm.
Pendulous fruit 20–75mm,
yellow, red or purplish, sweet
or acid-tasting. Cultivated
throughout Europe, often
naturalised in hedgerows.
This species includes several
different fruit trees. Plums
(subsp. *domestica*) have
greenish-white flowers and
large fruit longer than wide.
Bullace, Damsons and
Greengages (all subsp. *institia*)
have densely hairy, often
spiny twigs, pure white petals
and small or round fruit.

Wild Cherry *Prunus avium* Up
to 30m. Larger than most
other cherries, it has a well-
developed trunk with shiny,
red-brown bark peeling in
horizontal bands. Leaves 80–
150mm, oval to oblong,
abruptly pointed with blunt,
forward-pointing teeth;
undersides have prominent
veins with tufts of hairs in the
angles. Flowers April–May,
20–30mm diameter, appearing
just before leaves in clusters
of 2–6; 5 white petals 10–15mm
long. Fruits 9–12mm, long-
stalked; usually dark red,
sometimes yellowish, bright
red or black; sweet or bitter.
Common in mixed and
deciduous woods. Native
almost throughout Europe
and widely cultivated.

Roses

Sour Cherry *Prunus cerasus* Up to 8m. Round-headed tree or large shrub with a poorly defined, short or branched trunk. Suckers are often produced. Leaves 30–80mm slightly leathery, abruptly pointed at the tip, margins with small, rounded teeth; dark, glossy green above, the paler, prominently veined underside is downy when young, but becomes smooth. Flowers April–May, just before the leaves, in clusters of 2–6; 5 petals. Fruit 18mm, bright red; long-stalked, acid-tasting. Native to south-west Asia; introduced to Europe for the edible fruit, widely planted and naturalised in many places.

Japanese Cherry *Prunus serrulata* Up to 15m. The horizontal boughs of this small tree bear masses of delicately coloured blossom in spring. Bark reddish or purplish-brown, barred with distinctive horizontal bands of lenticels. Leaves 80–200mm, oval to inverted-oval; dark shiny green above, bluish below; long, tapering tip and sharp, long-pointed, spreading teeth. Flowers April–May, just before the leaves, in clusters of 2–4; white or pink and often double; 5 petals 15–40mm long, notched. Fruit dark, red-purple, rarely produced. Probably native to China; widely cultivated ornamental and street tree in Europe with many different forms.

Bird Cherry *Prunus padus* Up to 17m. The bark of this small tree is smooth, grey-brown and has a strong, unpleasant smell. Leaves 60–100mm, slightly leathery, dark green above, paler or bluish below; oblong-elliptical with a tapering point and sharply fine-toothed margin. Flowers May, appearing after leaves in elongated spikes of 70–150mm containing 15–35, white, almond-scented flowers; 5 petals 6–9mm long. Fruit 60–80mm, shiny black; tart, astringent. Grows in woods, thickets and hedgerows in damp soils and by streams in limestone areas. Native to most of Europe except the Mediterranean; sometimes planted for ornament.

Cherry Laurel *Prunus laurocerasus* Up to 8m. Small, spreading evergreen which has glossy, stiff and leathery leaves smelling of almonds when crushed. Young shoots green. Leaves 100–200mm, dark and glossy green above, yellowish-green below; oblong to lance-shaped with rolled-under, entire or minutely toothed margins. Flowers April, fragrant, in upright spikes equal in length to the leaves; 5 white petals, 4mm long. Fruit 20mm, red ripening shiny black. Native to the Balkan Peninsula but grown for ornament in much of Europe and commonly naturalised in open woods.

Peas

Judas-tree *Cercis siliquastrum* Up to 10m. This slender, spreading tree bears flowers directly on the trunk and main branches as well as on the twigs. Often several trunks. Crown thin and irregular. Leaves 70–120mm, almost circular, heart-shaped at base; bluish-green when young, turning dark or sometimes yellowish-green above. Flowers May, sometimes before the leaves; 15–20mm long; pink and pea-like. Pods 60–100mm, ripen purplish-brown. Native to the Mediterranean, but often grown as an ornamental elsewhere. It grows on dry, chalky soils in northern Europe, but is susceptible to the cold.

Carob *Ceratonia siliqua* Up to 10m. Domed and thickly branched, this bushy evergreen makes a low tree. Pinnate leaves have 2–5 pairs of leaflets, but no terminal leaflet; each leathery leaflet of 30–50mm is dark, shiny green above and pale below; the margins may be wavy. Flowers August–October; tiny, lacking petals, and are grouped in short, green spikes. Males and females may be borne on the same or on separate trees. Pods 100–200mm, violet-brown when ripe. Native to the drier parts of the Mediterranean where it is also grown for fodder.

Golden Wreath *Acacia saligna*
Up to 10m. In strings of small
pompoms, the tiny flowers of
this irregularly shaped and
drooping evergreen are bright
yellow. Small tree or shrub
with weeping twigs. Leaves
pendulous, variable in size and
shape, but usually 100–200mm
long and straight or sickle-
shaped; dull or shiny, with a
single vein. Flowers March–
May, grouped into spherical
heads 10–15mm diameter. Pods
60–120mm long and 4–8mm
wide are straight, narrow and
flattened, pinched between
each seed. Native to western
Australia, one of several *Acacia*
species used as sand
stabilisers; widely planted in
southern Europe.

Silver Wattle *Acacia dealbata* Up
to 30mm. Feathery and
delicate, the evergreen foliage
is silvery-hairy, especially
when young. Bark grey-green,
smooth. Leaves pinnately
divided, each division in turn
pinnately divided into leaflets
only 5mm long; more bluish
above than below. Flowers
January–March, the numerous
pale yellow, spherical heads 5–
6mm diameter. Pods 40–100mm
long and 10–12mm wide,
brown, flattened and only
slightly pinched between the
seeds. Native to south-east
Australia and Tasmania;
planted in southern Europe
mainly for timber and
ornament, it is the 'mimosa' of
florists; widely naturalised,
especially in the understory of
woods.

Peas

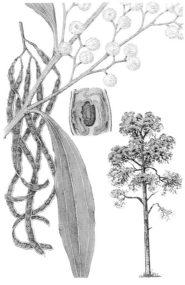

Blackwood *Acacia melanoxylon*
15–40m. Robust and very
erect, this rough-barked
evergreen rarely reaches its
maximum height. Bark
brown, furrowed. Leaves 60–
130mm, dull, dark green,
slightly curved, they have 3–5
prominent veins; feathery,
pinnately divided leaves
occasionally appear, especially
on young trees. Flowers July–
October, the creamy-white,
spherical heads 10mm
diameter. Pods 70–120mm long
and 8–10mm wide, red-brown;
flattened and twisted. The
seeds have conspicuous scarlet
stalks. Native to south-
eastern Australia and
Tasmania, planted for timber
and naturalised in south-west
Europe.

Laburnum *Laburnum anagyroides*
Up to 7m. Attractively decked
with flower-clusters in
summer, this small, slender
tree looks tattered in autumn
with the persistent husks of
the seed-pods. Branches
ascending or arching. Leaves
grey-green divided into 3
elliptical leaflets each 30–80mm
long. Flowers May–June, pea-
like, yellow and fragrant, in
pendulous clusters of 100–
300mm. Pods 40–60mm, smooth
and dark brown when ripe;
persist on trees after splitting,
exposing paler inner surfaces
and poisonous black seeds.
Short-lived tree of upland
woods and thickets. Native to
southern and central Europe;
widely planted ornamental,
often naturalised.

False Acacia *Robinia pseudacacia*
Up to 25m. The short, often
several, trunks of this open-
crowned tree have bark with
spiralling ridges and brittle,
twisted branches. Young
twigs dark red-brown, with
short thorny spines. Leaves
150–200mm, pinnate; 3–10 pairs
of yellowish-green leaflets,
each with tiny, leaf-like
growth at the base of the
stalk. Flowers June, white and
fragrant, pea-like, in dense,
hanging clusters 100–200mm
long. Smooth pods 50–100mm,
persist on tree for some time.
Native to open woods of
North America; widely
planted as a street and
amenity tree and now
naturalised, mainly in
southern Europe.

Sweet Orange *Citrus sinensis*
Up to 10m. Glossy-leaved,
almost shining, this rounded
evergreen tree bears both
flowers and fruit
simultaneously. Twigs spiny.
Leaves 75–100mm, elliptical;
dark, glossy green above, firm
and leathery, and dotted with
shiny oil glands. They have a
short, prominently winged
stalk. Flowers large, white and
fragrant; solitary or in loose
clusters and borne all year
round. Fruit is the well-
known orange, *c* 75mm
diameter, thick skinned with
sweet, juicy flesh. Native to
eastern Asia; grown in
orchards and gardens all
around the Mediterranean.
There are many similar
species, differing mainly in
their fruits.

Lemon *Citrus limon* Up to 10m. Similar in appearance to the Sweet Orange, this evergreen tree bears the familiar oval, pale yellow fruit. Leaves *c* 100mm, glossy green above; leathery with minutely toothed margins; usually a spine at the base of the short, winged leaf stalk. Flowers small and white, flushed purple on the outside; borne all year round. Fruit 65–125mm, oval with a protruding apex, yellow when ripe; juicy flesh remains sour. Origin obscure, but widely cultivated throughout the Mediterranean.

Tree-of-Heaven *Ailanthus altissima* 20–30m. The branches of this fast-growing tree are strongly ascending. Trunk very straight, suckering at the base. Bark grey. Leaves 450–600mm, rank-smelling, pinnate, usually ending with an odd leaflet. Leaflets 70–120mm, 2–4 small teeth near the base; unfolding red, becoming dark green above, paler beneath. Flowers July, 7–8mm diameter, 5 petals, greenish-white, strongly scented; males and females on separate trees. Fruits 30–40mm, with a twisted, membranous wing. Prefers dry, light soils; tolerant of air pollution, native to China; widely planted in Europe as a street tree and soil stabiliser, often naturalised.

Stag's-horn Sumach *Rhus typhina* Up to 10m. Covered with thick, velvety hair, the regularly forked branches of this small tree or shrub resemble deer antlers. Often suckering or with several trunks. Leaves pinnately divided into 11–29 drooping leaflets, each 50–120mm long; turn bright orange and red in autumn. Flowers May–July, greenish male and red female flowers usually on separate trees. Dense fruiting heads up to 200mm long are dull crimson, hairy and remain on the bare tree through winter. Native to North America but a common ornamental in Europe and naturalised in northern and central parts.

Pepper-tree *Schinus molle* Up to 12m. Reminiscent of a Weeping Willow, this graceful evergreen tree has slender, drooping twigs and long, hanging clusters of flowers and fruit. Leaves pinnately divided into 7–13 pairs of leaflets, usually ending in a point; leaflets each 20–60mm long and 3–8mm wide, smell of pepper when crushed. Flowers June–December; 4mm diameter; creamy, borne in loose clusters up to 250mm long. Fruit 7mm diameter, pink and bead-like. Mountain species, native to Central and South America. Grown as an ornamental in southern Europe and sometimes naturalised there.

Sumachs

Turpentine-tree *Pistacia terebinthus* 5-10m. Leaves of this small, grey-barked tree or shrub smell resinous and the twigs are stickily resinous too. Leaves pinnately divided and ending in a spine; 3-9 leathery, dark and shiny leaflets, each 20-85mm. Male and female flowers March–April, appearing with the leaves in dense green to brownish-purple clusters on separate trees; petals absent. Fruit 5-7mm, coral red when young, ripening brown. A species of scrub and thin woodland, preferring dry and rocky, chalky soils. Native to the Mediterranean, Portugal and south-west Asia.

Mastic-tree *Pistacia lentiscus* Up to 6m. Growing on dry, sunny slopes, this bushy and spreading evergreen tree has highly aromatic leaves and fruit. Twigs warty. Leaves have a winged stalk ending in a short spine; pinnately divided with 3-6 pairs of dark green, leathery leaflets, each 10-50mm long and 5-15mm wide. Flowers April, yellow-tinged to purplish, in dense, spiky heads in the leaf axils; petals absent. Aromatic fruit 4mm, bright red when young, ripening black. Found on rocky slopes, in open thickets and on the edges of woods. Native to the Mediterranean and Portugal.

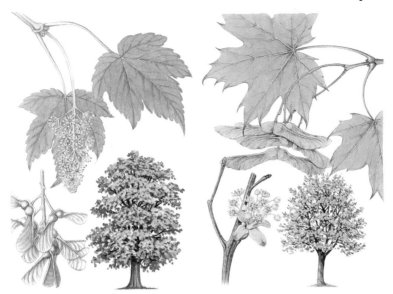

Sycamore *Acer pseudoplatanus*
Up to 35m. Scatttering its
winged fruit far and wide, this
large leaved tree can be a
rapid coloniser. Fast-growing,
crown often broader than
high. Bark flaking, dappled
light and dark reddish-brown.
Leaves opposite, varying in
size and lobing, usually 100–
150mm with 5 coarsely toothed
lobes. Flowers April,
appearing with leaves in
pendulous male or female
heads 60-120 long; 5 petals.
Dry fruit winged, borne in
pairs 60mm across. Native to
upland woods in central and
southern Europe, introduced
and widely naturalised in
many areas. Resistant to salt-
winds and air pollution.

Norway Maple *Acer platanoides*
Up to 30m. Similar to its close
relative the Sycamore, this
Maple is smaller but more
colourful in both spring and
autumn. Domed tree, trunk
often short. Bark greyish,
smooth or finely fissured.
Leaves 100-150mm, opposite,
with 5-7 lobes bearing large,
slender teeth. Flowers April,
before the leaves; 8mm
diameter, yellowish-green, 5
petals; in erect male or female
heads. Pairs of dry, winged
fruits 60-100mm across. Native
to upland forests and
deciduous woods in much of
Europe. It is often planted as
an ornamental and street tree,
especially in variegated-leaved
forms.

Macles

Field Maple *Acer campestre* Up to 25m. The pinkish young leaves of this small tree or shrub turn dark green in summer, then reddish or bright yellow in autumn. Crown domed; trunk twisting. Twigs develop corky flanges or wings. Leaves 40–120mm, opposite, rather thick; 3 upper lobes and often 2 smaller, basal lobes, all with rounded teeth towards tips. Flowers April or May, appearing with the leaves; 5 petalled; in erect heads containing both males and females. Fruit red-tinged, borne in clusters of 4 pairs, with horizontally spreading wings. Native to northern Europe, generally on chalky soils.

Box-elder *Acer negundo* Up to 20m. Numerous, twiggy sprouts grow from the trunk and branches of this fast-growing but short-lived tree. Opposite leaves 100–150mm, pinnately divided into 3, 5 or sometimes 7 oval leaflets; leaflets toothed, may also have 2–3 irregular lobes. Flowers March, appearing before the leaves on separate male and female trees; females greenish, but male flowers have conspicuous red anthers; petals absent. Dry fruit *c* 20mm, paired; slightly curved wings form an acute angle. Native to eastern North America; variegated forms are commonly planted as street trees and ornamentals; occasionally naturalised.

Red Maple *Acer rubrum* Up to
23m. A blaze of colour in
autumn, this fast-growing
maple also has red twigs,
buds, young leaves, flowers
and fruit. Branches ascending.
Leaves 80–100mm, opposite; 3–
5 shallow, coarsely toothed
lobes; initially reddish, turning
green above and silvery below
as they expand. Flowers
appear in March, before the
leaves; 5 petals. Dry fruit *c*
10mm, bright red; the wings of
each pair form a narrow
angle. Native to North
America but one of the most
widely planted maples in
Europe, especially on moist
soils along roadsides.

Horse-chestnut *Aesculus
hippocastanum* Up to 35m.
Magnificent spreading tree
with stout trunk, big divided
leaves and showy candles of
flowers. Large winter leaf-
buds up to 35mm are
extremely sticky. Opposite
leaves divided into 5–7 leaflets,
each 100–250mm long, which
spread like the fingers of a
hand. Flowers May; 4–5 frilled
white petals with pink or
yellow centres form erect
clusters or candles 150–300mm.
Fruit 60mm diameter, has one
or more shiny seeds, 'conkers',
enclosed in a leathery, spiny
case. Native to mountains in
central Balkan Peninsula, but
widely planted throughout
Europe, especially in parks and
avenues, and sometimes
naturalised.

Holly *Ilex aquifolium* 3–15m. An evergreen, with striking dark, prickly foliage contrasting with bright berries. Usually a small tree but often only a shrub. Bark, silver-grey, smooth, eventually becoming finely fissured. Leaves 50–120mm long, wavy and stiffly spined; dark green and very shiny above, much paler beneath. Flowers May–August, *c* 6mm diameter; 4 petals, white; males and females on separate trees, only males are fragrant. Berries 7–12mm, bright scarlet. Native throughout western and southern Europe, common in scrub, hedgerows and as a shrub layer in woods.

Spindle-tree *Euonymus europaeus* Up to 6m. Soft, matt pink, the curious fruit capsules of this otherwise rather inconspicuous tree split to reveal contrasting orange seeds. Normally a slender, twiggy tree or shrub. Young twigs are four-angled. Leaves 30–100mm, elliptic to oval, paired; medium to dark green in summer, colourful purplish-red in autumn. Flowers May–June; 4 narrow, greenish-yellow petals. Fruit 10–15mm diameter, a four-lobed capsule, each lobe containing a single seed. Lime-loving, growing in hedges, scrub and woodland margins. Native to most of Europe except far north and south; often planted for ornament.

Box *Buxus sempervirens* Up to 5m. Becoming rare in much of its native range, this evergreen tree or shrub is a widely planted ornamental. Young twigs four-angled, green with persistent white hairs. Leaves 15–30mm long, opposite, notched with rolled-down margins; dark and glossy above, pale green beneath, they have white hairs on the basal half. Flowers April, in tight clusters 5mm diameter; 5–6 male flowers surround a single female. All lack petals. Capsule *c* 7mm long, tipped with 3 spreading horns; explodes to disperse seeds. Scattered through western Europe on chalky soils.

Christ's Thorn *Paliurus spina-christi* Up to 3m. Formidably spiny, the numerous, clinging branches of this small tree or shrub form impenetrable barriers. Twigs flexible, zig-zagging, with pairs of spines, one hooked and one straight, all needle-sharp. Leaves 20–40mm, form two rows along the twig and may be either entire or minutely toothed. Flowers July, 5mm diameter; 5 petals, yellow. Woody fruits 20–30mm diameter; resemble broad-brimmed hats, the brim formed by a wavy, spreading wing. Native to hot, dry parts of the Mediterranean, especially the eastern end and the Balkan Peninsula; sometimes used for farm hedges.

Buckthorns

Buckthorn *Rhamnus catharticus*
4–10m. Opposite, spiny
branches, spreading at right
angles, produce short, lateral
shoots which bear the leaves
and flowers. Leaves 30–70mm,
in opposite pairs at 90° to each
other; upper leaf surface dull
green, lower pale green with
2–4 pairs of conspicuous
lateral veins curving towards
leaf-tip. Flowers May–June;
4mm, fragrant; males and
females on separate trees; 4 or
rarely 5 tiny greenish-white
petals. Fruit 6–8mm diameter,
berry-like; ripens black.
Common on chalky soils, in
hedges, scrub and deciduous
woods. Native to all of Europe
but the Mediterranean region.

Alder-buckthorn *Frangula alnus*
Up to 5m. Folding downwards
on the twigs prior to falling in
autumn, the leaves of this
small tree will have already
turned shiny, bright yellows
and reds. Branches ascend at a
sharp angle. Leaves 20–70mm,
entire; 7–9 pairs of lateral
veins curving towards wavy
leaf margins. Flowers May–
June; 3mm across, with 5 tiny
greenish-white petals. Fruit 6–
10mm diameter; berry-like;
ripens from green through
yellow and red to purplish-
black. Common in hedges,
woods and bogs in much of
Europe; absent from far north
and some parts of the
Mediterranean.

Large-leaved Lime *Tilia platyphyllos* Up to 40m. Attracted by copious nectar from the sweet-smelling flowers, bees swarm around this earliest flowering of limes. Narrowly domed with ascending branches. Leaves 60–90mm, green-hairy, especially beneath; heart-shaped. Flowers June, in long-stalked, pendulous clusters containing 2–6, 5-petalled, yellowish and fragrant flowers attached to whitish, wing-like bract. Nut, 8–12mm, globose, hairy; 3–5 prominent ribs. Native to hills with damp, rich soils in central and southern Europe, planted as a street tree in other areas.

Small-leaved Lime *Tilia cordata* Up to 32m. Arching downwards, the branches of this tree form a dense, domed cone. Leaves 30–90mm, heart-shaped; they have tufts of pale red-brown hairs in the axils of the veins beneath. Flowers July, in pendulous clusters; 4–15, translucent, 5-petalled, white, fragrant flowers are attached to a pale green, wing-like bract. Nut 6mm, thin-shelled, globose, downy at first but becomes smooth and is usually ribbed. Native to limestone areas in much of Europe except the far north and south; often planted as a street tree.

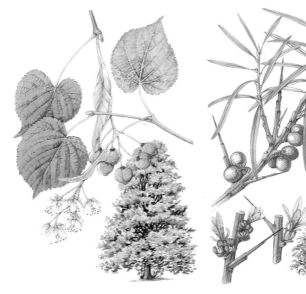

Common Lime *Tilia* x *vulgaris*
Up to 46m. Prone to aphid and
fungal attack, the leaves of
this tall tree drip sticky sap.
Branches begin low on trunk
and give a narrow crown.
Leaves 60–100mm, broad, cut
almost straight across at the
base; undersides have tufts of
white hairs in the angles of
the veins. Flowers July; each
long-stalked, pendant cluster
of 5–10 yellow-white, 5-
petalled, fragrant flowers is
attached to a yellowish-green,
wing-like bract. Nut 8mm,
thick-shelled, ovoid to
globose, downy and weakly
ribbed. Of hybrid origin,
widely used as a street and
park tree.

Sea-buckthorn *Hippophae
rhamnoides* Up to 11m. A
sprawling spiny shrub in
exposed places but forms a
densely branched tree in
sheltered sites. Numerous
suckers grow from the base of
the trunk. Twigs and leaves
covered with tiny silvery
scales. Leaves 10–60mm long
and 3–10mm wide, grey-green
above, silvery below; narrow,
stalkless. Flowers March–
April, before the leaves, on
separate male and female
trees; 2 tiny green sepals, no
petals. Berries 6–8mm, orange,
oval. Native to much of
Europe, mainly on cliffs and
sand dunes, sometimes inland;
planted as a sand-binder and
ornamental, often naturalised
in open sites.

Oleaster *Elaeagnus angustifolia*
Up to 13m. Resembling Sea-
buckthorn, with an even more
silvery appearance, this tree is
larger and only occasionally
spiny. Young twigs silver and
shining, becoming dark and
smooth with age. Leaves 40–80
long and 10–25mm wide; they
are densely silver-hairy
beneath. Flowers June,
appearing with the young
leaves; fragrant; silvery
outside, yellow within, they
have 4 sepals but no petals.
Fleshy oval berries, 10–20mm,
are also scattered with silver
scales. Native to western Asia,
grown in central and southern
Europe for ornament and for
the edible fruits; sometimes
naturalised.

Tamarisk *Tamarix gallica* Up to
8m. Slender, feathery foliage
gives this much-branched
small evergreen tree or shrub
a diffuse and open look. Bark
dark purple or almost black.
Tiny leaves of 1.5–2mm clasp
the twigs. Flowers are 5-
petalled, pink or white, tiny
and crowded into long slender
spikes only 3–5mm wide. Tiny
capsules release seeds tufted
with hair. Native to south-
west Europe; often cultivated
and sometimes naturalised.
There are 7 similar species of
Tamarisk native to Europe;
all are resistant to salt winds
and several are planted as
ornamentals, usually near
the sea, and may become
naturalised.

Myrtles

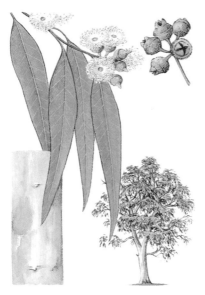

Red Gum *Eucalyptus camaldulensis* Up to 40m. Blue juvenile leaves precede very different pale green adult leaves on this short-trunked, spreading evergreen tree. Juvenile leaves 60–90mm, stalked, waxy; opposite for 3–4 pairs, then alternate. Adult leaves 120–220mm, conspicuously veined. Flowers December–February; white, in clusters of 7–11; buds have conical lids. Woody fruit 6–8mm, opens by means of 4 sharp teeth. Native to Australia, probably the most widely grown of all the Eucalyptus species planted in Europe and cultivated for timber on a large scale on heavy soils in the Mediterranean region.

Tasmanian Blue Gum *Eucalyptus globulus* Up to 65m. Shredding bark forms patterns of pale grey, white and yellow on the thick trunks of this tall evergreen. Juvenile leaves 70–160mm, blue; opposite, forming numerous, spreading, stalkless pairs. Adult leaves 100–300mm, green and leathery; alternate, narrower, sickle-shaped and stalked. Flowers September–December, in clusters of 1–3, the buds with pointed lids. Fruit 15–30mm, waxy and distinctly ribbed, woody; opens by 3–6 valves. Native to south-east Australia and Tasmania; a source of timber, paper and eucalyptus oil in southern Europe where it is widely planted on hillsides, and an ornamental elsewhere.

Cider Gum *Eucalyptus gunnii* Up to 30m. Disc-like pairs of juvenile leaves threaded on long slender shoots are produced during the first four or so years by this slender open evergreen. Bark flaking, reveals green, white and pinkish patches. Juvenile leaves 30–40mm, blue; opposite, rounded and stalkless. Adult leaves 40–70mm, green; alternate. Flowers January–February; club-shaped flower-buds borne in threes. Fruit 7–10mm, opens by 3–5 teeth set in a depressed disc on the top. Native to Tasmania, fast-growing highland species widely planted in cooler parts of Europe, mainly for its ornamental juvenile foliage.

Pomegranate *Punica granatum* Up to 8m. Crumpled scarlet flowers with numerous stamens tip the slender, glossy-leaved twigs of this small tree. Branches ascending or erect, may be spiny. Leaves 20–80mm, opposite, entire, oblong-lanceolate or widest above the middle. Flowers June–September; 25–40mm diameter; solitary or in pairs; sepal tube has usually 5 thick, pointed lobes; 5–7 petals, scarlet or occasionally white. Globular fruit 50–80mm, leathery, yellow or reddish, contains many seeds embedded in translucent purplish pulp. Native to south-west Asia, cultivated in southern Europe for edible fruit; naturalised in parts of the Mediterranean.

Cornelian Cherry *Cornus mas*
Up to 8m. Dense clusters of
flowers appear in spring on
the bare, downswept twigs of
this small trees of shrub.
Crown very open, with
spreading branches. Opposite
leaves 40–100mm, yellowish-
green, conspicuously veined.
Flowers February–March,
appearing before the leaves;
each 4-petalled flower is 4mm
across; bright yellow. Fleshy
berry 6mm, bright red, acid-
tasting. In thickets and woods
on all but acid soils. Native to
central and south-eastern
Europe, also cultivated for
fruit and for ornament.

Strawberry-tree *Arbutus unedo*
Up to 9m. Cinnamon-red bark
hangs in strips from the short
trunk of this dense, rounded
evergreen tree. Young twigs
red and glandular-hairy.
Leaves 40–110mm, glossy;
sharp, irregular teeth, those
towards tip tinged red.
Flowers and fruit borne
simultaneously; drooping
clusters of greenish- or
pinkish-white, urn-shaped
flowers each 9mm long
appearing October–November
alongside previous years'
berries, which are 20mm
diameter, globose, warty and
deep red when ripe. Native to
the Mediterranean in
evergreen scrub, and to
western Europe as far north
as Ireland, where it occurs in
young oakwoods.

Manna Ash *Fraxinus ornus* Up to 24m. Large, showy clusters of creamy-white, fragrant flowers adorn this tree as it comes into full leaf. Crown domed, regular. Bark grey, smooth. Grey or brown winter buds have a white bloom. Leaves up to 300mm, paired, pinnately divided into 5-9 irregularly toothed leaflets each 30-100mm long. Flowers May; in large clusters 150-200mm long; 4 narrow petals 5-6mm long. Slender, winged fruits 15-25mm, hang in dense clusters. Native to central and southern Europe; widely planted as a street tree; cultivated in Italy for the sweet, sticky, edible gum known as manna.

Common Ash *Fraxinus excelsior* Up to 40m. Tiny flowers emerging from fat, black winter buds give this tree a purplish tint in spring, before it bursts into leaf. Crown open, domed. Bark grey, smooth, eventually develops interwoven ridges. Leaves 200-350mm, paired, pinnately divided into 7-13 toothed leaflets, each 15-120mm, long. Flowers April–May, before the leaves, males and females often on separate twigs. Both sexes are purple and lack petals. Winged fruits of 25-50mm form dense, hanging clusters. Common everywhere, but growing best on deep, damp, alkaline soils. Native throughout Europe, also widely planted.

Olives

Narrow-leaved Ash *Fraxinus angustifolia* Up to 25m. Very narrow leaflets and coffee-coloured winter buds distinguish this tree from the larger Common Ash. The crown is irregularly domed. Bark becomes bubbly and warty, dark grey. Winter buds are hairy. Leaves 150–250mm, paired, pinnate with 5–13 long-pointed leaflets each 30–90mm long. Leaflets of older trees are much narrower than those of younger trees. Flowers in May appear before the leaves, bisexual and lacking petals. Winged fruits of 20–45mm hang in small clusters. Native to damp woods and flood plains in southern and south-east Europe.

Olive *Olea europaea* Up to 15m. Thick, gnarled and silvery, the trunk and main branches of this long-lived evergreen are pitted with large cavities and holes. Wild trees (var. *sylvestris*) are bushy and spiny; cultivated trees (var. *europaea*) are unarmed. Leathery leaves 20–80mm; grey-green above, silvery-hairy beneath; opposite. Flowers July–August in loose spikes; fragrant; 4-petalled. Fruit 10–35mm, green in first year ripens black in second; oily-fleshed, contains a single large stone. Native to southern Europe in lightly wooded, rocky areas; an important crop since ancient times, it is the source of olive oil.

Lilac *Syringa vulgaris* 3–7m.
Flowering profusely in early
summer, this tree or shrub
suckers freely and often forms
tall, very twiggy thickets.
Leaves 40–80mm, in opposite
pairs; may be oval or heart-
shaped; yellowish, slightly
leathery. In May or June the
shoots are tipped with showy,
fragrant, conical flowerheads
100–200mm long. Flowers
fleshy, tubular, with 4
spreading lobes; usually lilac,
but may be white or cream in
garden plants; always very
fragrant. Capsule *c* 10mm,
oval, brown. Native to rocky,
scrub-covered hillsides in the
Balkan Peninsula but widely
cultivated for ornament and
naturalised in other parts of
Europe.

Glossy Privet *Ligustrum lucidum*
Up to 15m. Familiar as a dense
garden hedge, this evergreen
forms a tree when left
unclipped. Branches spreading,
twigs flecked with white
pores. Leaves 80–120mm,
opposite; thick, dark and very
glossy above, paler and matt
beneath. Flowers August–
September or even later, in
loose cones of 120–200mm;
small, white, 4-lobed; have a
heavy scent. Oval berries of *c*
10mm are black with a white
bloom. Native to China;
widely used in southern
Europe as a hedge,
ornamental and street tree.
Other species are common as
hedging plants in northern
Europe.

Bignonias

Indian Bean-tree *Catalpa bignonioides* Up to 20m. Hanging from the otherwise bare twigs, the long, bean-like capsules of this tree are particularly noticeable in winter. Leaves 100–250mm, paired or rarely in whorls of 3; pale green or sometimes purple-tinged when young. Flowers June–August, in conical clusters; 50mm diameter, with 5 frilled white petals spotted with yellow and purple. Pendulous fruit capsules of 150–400mm long and less than 10mm wide contain flat, papery seeds. Native to south-eastern North America. The commonest of several similar species grown as ornamentals and street trees in southern and western Europe.

Foxglove-tree *Paulownia tomentosa* 12–26m. Sparse branches hung with huge leaves and large, tubular flowers make this tree a striking ornamental. Twigs purplish, dotted with warty pores. Leaves 450mm long and 250mm wide, opposite; grey felted beneath; in young trees they may have several shallow, tapering lobes. Flowers appear in May, before the leaves, in erect clusters 200–300mm; violet flowers up to 60mm have a long tube coloured yellow within and ending in 5 spreading lobes. Capsules 50mm, glossy and sticky; have a tapering tip. Native to China; common in gardens, sometimes planted as a street tree in southern Europe.

Elder *Sambucus nigra* Up to 10m. The plate like flower clusters of this small, bushy tree are headily fragrant but the leaves smell unpleasant. Main branches curve but vigorous straight shoots often grow from base. Bark grey or light brown, grooved and corky. Leaves opposite, pinnately divided into 5-7 leaflets each 45-120mm long. Flowers June–July; individually small but massed into showy, flat-topped heads 100-240mm diameter; 5-petalled, white. Berries 6-8mm, black when fully ripe. Common in open woods, hedgerows and on waste ground where soil is disturbed and nitrogen rich. Native throughout Europe.

Guelder-rose *Viburnum opulus* Up to 4m. Reminiscent of hydrangeas, the white flowerheads of this spreading tree have large sterile flowers surrounding much smaller fertile flowers. Leaves 30-80mm, opposite; downy beneath; 3 or 5 irregularly toothed lobes. Flowers June–July, the circular heads 45-105mm diameter with sterile flowers of 15-20mm around the rim and fertile flowers of only 4-7mm in the centre; 5-petalled, white. Fruit 8mm translucent red; may persist on the tree long after leaves have fallen. Native to most of Europe, in moist wood margins, thickets and hedges.

Honeysuckles

Wayfaring-tree *Viburnum lantana* Up to 6m. Found mainly on chalky soils, this small spreading tree or shrub brightens hedgerows and downland pastures with its flowers and berries. Leaves 40–140mm, opposite, rough, shortly toothed and grey-green with starry hairs, especially beneath. Flowers May–June in many-flowered heads 60–100mm diameter; 5 small white petals. Fruits 8mm oval; red ripening suddenly but not simultaneously to black, so that each fruiting head is two-coloured. Grows in hedgerows and on the fringes of woods. Native to Europe as far north as Britain and Sweden.

Laurustinus *Viburnum tinus* Up to 7m. Flowering in winter when few other trees are in bloom, this dense evergreen has attractive pink and white flowers. Leaves 30–100mm, opposite, entire and narrowly to very broadly oval in outline; dark, slightly glossy, thinly hairy beneath. Flowers appear in February and may continue to June, in clusters of 40–90mm diameter; 5 petals, pale pink outside and white within. Fruit small, metallic blue. Mainly found in woods and thickets on stony soils. Native to the Mediterranean region but frequently grown as an ornamental elsewhere.

Cabbage-tree *Cordyline australis*
Up to 13m. The bare, forked
trunks of this palm-like
evergreen are topped with
dense tufts of narrow, sword-
shaped leaves. Trunks fork
after flowering and often
sucker, forming clumps.
Leaves 300–900mm, hard and
sharp-pointed; dark green
often tinged yellow. Flowers
June or July; creamy-white,
fragrant, forming a huge,
branched cluster of 60–120cm
which grows from the centre
of the crown. Berries only
6mm diameter, blue-white.
Native to New Zealand, quite
hardy and a popular
ornamental and street tree in
southern and western Europe
but only near coasts.

European Fan Palm *Chamaerops
humilis* Up to 2m. This dwarf
palm has stiff, fan-shaped
leaves surmounting a thick,
fibre-covered trunk which
rarely grows more than 2m
high and is often completely
absent. Leaves 1m diameter;
green, greyish or bluish;
deeply divided into narrow
segments; old leaf bases
persist among white or grey
fibres on trunk. Yellow
flowers March–June, in a
dense spike hidden among the
leaves; males and females
usually on separate trees.
Globose fruits 45mm diameter,
yellow or brown. The only
common native palm in
Europe, mainly found in sandy
coastal regions of the western
Mediterranean.

Palms

Canary Island Date Palm
Phoenix canariensis Up to 20m.
Stout, unbranched and
scarred from old leaf-stalks,
the trunk of 1.5m diameter
bears a dense crown of many
feathery fronds. Leaves reach
5-6m long; pinnately divided
into numerous, narrow
leaflets and viciously spiny
towards the base of the stalk.
Flowers March–May; the
massive creamy-yellow
clusters reach 2m long.
Equally large clusters of dry,
inedible orange fruits hang
down from the crown. Native
to the Canary Islands, often
planted for ornament in
streets, parks and leisure
areas in the Mediterranean
region and south-west
Europe.

Chinese Windmill Palm
Trachycarpus fortunei Up to 14m.
The brown and shaggy trunk
of this palm is covered with
matted fibrous bases of dead
leaves, at least on the upper
part near the crown. Leaves
up to 1m, fan-shaped, divided
almost to the base into stiff,
narrow, pleated segments;
long stalks are fibrous at the
base. Fragrant, yellow flowers
March–June in many-
branched, conical clusters.
Fruit *c* 20mm, three-lobed
purplish-white. Native to
China. Ornamental along
roads and avenues, mainly in
the Mediterranean region but
quite hardy and grown as far
north as southern England.

Further Reading

Bean, W.J., *Trees and Shrubs Hardy in the British Isles*, eighth edition, vols I–IV & Supplement. John Murray, London, 1970–88.

Blombery, A. and Rodd T., *Palms*. Angus & Robertson, London, 1984.

Dallimore, W. and Jackson, A.B., *A Handbook of Coniferae and Ginkgoaceae*, fourth edition. Arnold, London, 1966.

Elliot, W.R. and Jones, D.L., *Encyclopaedia of Australian Plants Suitable for Cultivation*, vols I–IV. Lothian, Melbourne, 1980–6.

Krussman, G., *Manual of Cultivated Broad-leaved Trees and Shrubs*, vols I–III. Batsford, London, 1984–6.

Krussman, G., *Manual of Cultivated Conifers*. Timber Press, Portland, Oregon, 1985.

Phillips, R., *Trees of Britain, Europe and North America*. Pan, London, 1978.

Phillips, R. and Rix, M., *Shrubs*. Pan, London, 1989.

Polunin, O. and Everard, B., *Trees and Bushes of Europe*. Oxford University Press, London, 1976.

Tutin, T.G. *et al.* (editors), *Flora Europaea*, vols I–V. Cambridge University Press, Cambridge, 1964–80.

Vicomte de Noailles and Lancaster, R., *Mediterranean Plants and Gardens*. Floraprint, Nottingham, 1977.

Major Collections of Trees to Visit

Batsford Arboretum, Moreton-in-Marsh, Gloucestershire.

Bicton Gardens, East Budleigh, Devon.

Cambridge University Botanic Garden, Cambridge.

Castlewellan, Newcastle, Co. Down, Northern Ireland.

Dawyck Arboretum, Stobo, Peebles, Scotland.

Dyffryn Gardens, Dyffryn House, St Nicholas, Cardiff, South Glamorgan.

Granada Arboretum, Nantwich, Chesire.

Glasnevin Botanic Gardens, Dublin, Eire.

Hillier Arboretum, Ampfield, Hampshire.

Muncaster Castle, Ravenglass, Cumbria.

National Pinetum, Bedgebury, Kent.

Tresco Abbey Gardens, Tresco, Isles of Scilly.

Royal Botanic Garden, Edinburgh, Scotland.

Royal Botanic Gardens, Kew, Richmond-upon-Thames, Surrey.

Westonbirt Arboretum, Tetbury, Gloucestershire.

Wisley Gardens, Woking, Surrey.

Index

Index

Index